FIR WINDS TO
YOU ALL.

fred

The Sailing Game

Life in the Sailboat World

THE SAILING GAME

Life in the Sailboat World

by

Fred van Zuiden

Published in 2004 by:

G.B. Batteries Ltd.
#609, 3339 Rideau Place SW
Calgary, AB, Canada T2S 1Z5
email: vanzuiden@agt.net

Library and Archives Canada Cataloguing in Publication

Van Zuiden, Fred, 1930-
          The sailing game : life in the sailboat world / Fred van Zuiden ; editor, Gayl Veinotte.

 ISBN 0-9736870-0-2

1. Glenmore Sailboats Ltd. 2. Van Zuiden, Fred, 1930-. 3. Boatbuilding—Alberta—Calgary—History. 4. Boatbuilders—Alberta—Calgary—Biography. I. Veinotte, Gayl, 1950- II. Title.

HD9993.B633C36 2004   338.7'6238223'09712338   C2004-906426-6

Layout and Design: Gayl Veinotte
Printed in Calgary, Alberta, CANADA

Cover photo courtesy Bill Russell

This book is dedicated to
sailing enthusiasts around the world.

Table of Contents

The Sailing Game

Life in the Sailboat World

Foreword

If you were to ask me why I was writing, I would say that, besides making a living, I have experienced too many exciting, dramatic, and intense events over the past forty years to let them go to waste. Behind-the-scenes politics, a trucker in bone-numbing cold who stopped to help, a 300-pounder vehemently denying that he caused a flood in our washroom, a moan for help from a thief stuck in the chimney, and so much more. There were traumas while flying to regattas, bomb explosions, fork lifts piercing the plane, and close financial disasters. The warmth of customers appearing with wine to share their sailing adventures is what spurred me on.

Thanks to those who helped change my Dutch grammar and long windedness into fine English: laptops don't catch all the errors. Writing forced me into the computer age, and I gained a great sense of well being from the process. Duuk van Heel and Hans Kreuz gave me a glimpse of international racing, and a feel of the wider world came from catamaran guru Hobie Alter and Laser factory head Steve Clark, also a Little America Cup victor. Last but not least, Fie Hulsker gave the low down on what it takes to be a sailing team manager.

These interviews gave me a much greater insight into the sailing world and my life, a world which continues to keep my muscles, bones, lungs, and brains operating at full speed!

The Sailing Game

Life in the Sailboat World

Chapter 1

Sailing and Racing

By Sheer Chance

In the summer of 1957, I lay on a beach at Vancouver's English Bay, having just arrived from Toronto in a bright new Dodge. I was teased about its lemon colour, but that's what it turned out to be. Lionel Stanpiros was sunning next to me, and we talked about my youth in war-torn Holland. I had emigrated in 1952, when I was twenty-one.

Lionel was an independent battery manufacturer and, after a few lunches, he surprised me with a job offer—would I open a sales operation in Calgary and when could I leave? This 670-mile (1100-km) surprise immediately caught my imagination. I worked in the Vancouver plant for a few weeks, learning about automotive and industrial batteries; at the age of 27 I hardly knew what a battery was.

We left in July, and Lionel rented premises in a downtown low rent district. I began making sales trips deep into Alberta and Eastern British Columbia at a time when they were still building highways through the Rockies. I made an average of twenty calls a day to construction camps out in the wilds and fell in love with the Canadian Rockies. The orders started coming in very nicely, and by the early sixties, the plant could not keep up with my sales. I hated telling customers I couldn't deliver when I knew they had costly construction equipment down.

Lionel told me to go skiing or take Wednesdays off, but I did not survive the horrors of war only to pursue pleasure, and besides, the Dutch work ethic had been pumped into me but good. He gave permission to get a sideline.

It so happened that I had recently had a sailing catamaran made, and several friends wanted one. It had been poorly built, so I got the North American rights from the British builder, and, one might say, a sideline fell into my lap.

In 1958, I met Audrey skiing in Banff, and three months later we married. Lionel, by now a close friend, was our best man.

How It Really All Started

In 1962, my friend Sandor Baksa who had escaped the 1956 Hungarian Revolution persuaded me to go 50-50 on a used 16 ft. (4.88 m) Falcon sailboat. I think it came out of *Popular Mechanics* and was beamy, with a roomy, deep cockpit. I discovered its shortcomings later, but on the face of it, $150 seemed a good deal for this perky white boat and trailer.

Audrey, ever the practical one, said "you can't sail!" So, we went to the library for a basic how-to-sail book and a cheque was written. We were not hindered in those days with trailer licenses, insurance, boating certificates, and a million other bureaucratic niceties.

We took the Falcon out in a light breeze, and to this day I recommend newcomers start out in 3 to 5 mph. (5 to 8 km/h) winds. Audrey sat with the book; I manned the tiller; and we tried to figure out where the wind was and how to set the sails to go faster. It was a classic little boat and it taught us how to raise a mast, boom and sails, and how to use the ropes, fittings, and rudder.

Glenmore Reservoir is Calgary's foremost water supply. It had been a make-work project in the "dirty thirties" and is roughly three miles long and one mile wide (5 km x 1 km). Having this lake in our midst was the principal reason so many citizens of this landlocked city got into sailing, and in the early sixties the city started a sailing school and rescue service.

The reservoir is vulnerable to severe western winds funneling in from Lake Minnewanka and Ghost, not to mention the Chinooks. Weather forecasts were not very sophisticated then,

Our first sailboat was a Falcon named Luctor et Ermergo

and we relied on a black ball being hoisted when it was unsafe to sail. The tricky winds at Glenmore made good sailors of all of us. We learned quickly to survey water colour to judge wind strength and, in one dreadful storm, our little Falcon rescued a sailor yelling for help; we also learned about hypothermia.

Our Falcon took on water each weekend, and we had to tar between the slats in the cockpit or lay tarred hemp, an age-old method. Soon, we had a completely tarred bottom and were getting heavier by the week. Our sailing partner was using the docks to stop the boat, and the centre board and rudder were forever being rebuilt.

It is true what they say about sharing a wife, car, or a sailboat, so we bought Sandor out. Strangely, the cheque never went through, even though he got his money. We put our dear Falcon up for sale and took an eastside Chestermere lake lot on trade. The lot had many trees, but was mosquito rich. Anxious for our money, we shortly sold our real estate for a handsome $1,000, only to be disillusioned in the nineties when these lots went, without a blink, for over half a million.

In the days we sailed the Falcon, British Yachting World 15 ft. 6 in. (4.65 m) catamarans went whizzing by us. It did not take long for this performance to intrigue me, and I realized that catamarans had come of age. The Yachting World had fibreglass u-shaped displacement hulls and lots of sail at 175 sq. ft. (16.26 m2) and a PYR rating of 78.

Bringing in a different catamaran seemed foolhardy, but a

geologist friend, Hubert Steghaus, highly recommended the British 16 ft. (4.88 m) Flying Kitten (FK), which was being built by Tony Robb on Shuswap Lake, British Columbia.

The Flying Kitten Catamaran

We took a huge leap and ordered a Flying Kitten, whose design is still unique. There were few planing-hulled catamarans about, but the Flying Kitten spanned the performance crown in a good wind. Designed by F. M. Montgomery of Falmouth, England, using Mosquito bomber principles, she was partially made of sitka spruce found in the rainy coastal ranges of British Columbia, and Dutch Bruynzeel mahogany. Her weight was low at 300 lbs. (136 kg) with 178 sq. ft. (16.5 m2) of fully battened mainsail.

We drove 683 miles (1,100 km) to Tony for the first test sail, only to have her thin mast literally explode in a moderate 9 mph. (14.5 km/h) wind, so home we went. Tony assured us it was now ready and we made the long drive a second time, only to go home empty handed. On the third try, we found this attractive catamaran just about ready!

Fred on the Flying Kitten Catamaran

Life in the Sailboat World

We did the maiden launch on Glenmore, and, unbelievably, the mast broke. My patience broke, too. I called the British designer, and he agreed to have Holt Allen supply aluminum spars by air. Air freight was a problem those days, as few planes in the mid-sixties could accommodate 24 feet (7.3 m) in the hold.

F & A Builders, our first designated boat company, would henceforth build the Flying Kitten in Canada with aluminum spars, and our sideline jumped into action. We had Hans Stammer build ten Flying Kittens in his garage, and we also sold six kits. These were proudly offered along with Holt Allan spars, Windward Sails, and all the fittings, foils, glues, nails, and screws a home-based builder would ever need. It was highly unusual to find such a complete kit and unique in Calgary.

With our technically faster and lighter Flying Kitten, we were soon beating the Yachting Worlds. Hubert Steghaus was still helping us promote and told me about a young, blond, very bright immigrant from Germany who was looking for a crewing job. I made contact with Hans Kreuz and a delightful sailing/working relationship developed, lasting many decades.

Hans, as crew, was soon teaching me how to find the wind, set the sails, and tune the boat. He taught me the principles by likening sailing to two hand palms folded together. He showed how to propel our cat higher and higher into the wind by playing the puffs and hiking violently, which gained us many inches to windward. He explained the mysteries of weather and lee helm and how to induce or eliminate it by working with rudder, daggerboard angles, and sitting position. Adjusting the mast forward is necessary in severe cases. He advised me never to have a heavy tiller that needed fighting.

Lee helm happens when the boat sails away from the wind and you need to move the mast back quickly. A slight weather helm is good, as it will turn the boat back to you if you fall off. Countless times a boat will sail away, only to come to a stop on some far away shore. I have seen a good few champions left gasping in the water because their boats had neutral helm, which was faster, but oh, the price they paid! Do yourselves a favour and get your boat properly tuned, even if it involves new standing rigging. It's a small price to pay.

Remember: wearing a personal floatation device (PFD) in the water handicaps your ability to swim, but you must stay with the boat. In rough weather you cannot be seen easily, so staying with the boat stops you from becoming an unfortunate statistic. While PFDs are vital, besides impeding swimming, they are a possible deathtrap if you are caught under a sail, cat trampoline, or deck, because you can't dive away from underneath unless you remove your jacket. I recommend vests that can be unzipped quickly or are fastened with Velcro. Sometimes people get caught in the rigging, and I recommend carrying a knife — a perfect Christmas present. As an aside, dogs cannot swim under water as they can't hold their breath, but if their heads are kept up with a doggie PFD, it helps them to keep their noses above water.

Hans also taught when to tack and to do it fast, to sit forward in light and moderate winds, to lift the transom out of the water to decrease drag, and to carve one's battens to achieve proper airfoil. The total curve or draft should be one third of the overall length of the batten, and the deepest point one quarter of the overall length. He explained sail settings, when to flatten, and when to hollow. He insisted on sails being set neither too tight nor too loose, and kept testing them by letting off the sheet continually. In short, he taught proper sailing, which he seemed to do with a natural ease and grace. He also emphasized taking advantage of the Cunningham, the Highfield lever, and the ever important foils. He thought it important to keep your eyes on the burgee and to change seating continuously to decrease drag. Catamarans need to have the weather hull just kiss the water and not rise up in the air as so many cowboys like to do.

Hans and I found ourselves winning or, at worst, placing second in club and provincial races on both straight or handicap time. Hans was the cause of all this, and I turned over the FK to his captaincy. Our strategy was to gain even more potential with Hans coaching me to power the jib. It worked, and winning became a sweet habit.

Around this time, we became aware that there was a prejudice against catamarans or some kind of anti-multihull syndrome, and I must admit that in its own subtle way it is still out there. It meant nothing that there had been a multihull class in the Olympics for over 30 years and major world class ocean races. Our catamaran was often ridiculed, and we would respond to good-natured clients that it was too bad some people liked half-boats, or that there were more monohull wrecks on the ocean bottoms than multihulls.

Detail of a deck with its jungle of ropes

There were soon enough FKs for class racing, and we often had starts with a dozen or more. Men like Hubert Steghaus, Jim Kirker, Ed Schulz, and Mike Baxter suddenly started giving Hans and I tough competition. We organized racing on Sylvan Lake, near Red Deer, and brought markers to set a course. I can still feel the exhilaration of sailing in good prairie winds, scooping water out of the lake to slake our thirst. Try doing that in these days of polluted water! We also ventured outside Alberta to sanctioned racing in places like Kelowna and Saskatoon. The sailing world has its share of prima donnas, too, and I remember on one of these trips a sailor screaming his displeasure at being beaten and drumming the cockpit with his fists, as if to blame the boat.

In 1967, we heard about the Worlds Multihull Championship, slated for Long Beach, California. We decided to make the trek and test our FK against other catamaran designs. We built a new FK, bought new British sails, and worked on our battens for hours to get the one-third / one-quarter formula to achieve a truly vertical wing shape. We spent another 400 man-hours finishing the paint surface. We did the underwater ship in gun-metal grey graphite, which was so slick, Hans said a fly landing on it would break its legs. The hours of dedication needed to compete internationally really came home to us. We tested ourselves in local races and found our winning margin had further improved.

Our anticipation built every day at the prospect of this exciting trip, and we suffered angst as to whether our Mosquito-bomber-inspired catamaran could be a winning sensation in what is still the heart of catamaran sailing in California. Our expedition took us through Montana, Idaho, and Nevada. It was terribly hot in the Nevada desert, and having the convertible top down was almost too much for us erstwhile Europeans. We went through powerful rainstorms where the skies split open so fast there was no time to get the top up.

In Las Vegas, we pulled up to Caesar's Palace and faced the austere doorman with bravado, sun-browned faces, wild, blowing hair, and a strange boat in tow. Our hippie look was enough to deny us accommodations, so we stayed at the much friendlier Sands. Once in Los Angeles, we marvelled at all the sailboat dealers and found Larry Bacon, who sold the Aqua Cat. His yard had all manner of catamarans—a veritable candy shop for us landlocked sailors. Larry feigned interest in our FK, but thought our wide 2 ft. (.73 m) transoms would not work in Pacific coast wave conditions. We had a little surprise in store for him.

Life in the Sailboat World

Observing these trials was exciting and something completely new to us. We were told we would be tested in a straight line between two buoys and then around regular buoy courses. There must have been about a hundred different multihulls, and some classes had more than one entry. For the first time, we saw the massive C Class with 300 sq. ft. (28 m2) and D Class with 500 sq. ft. (46 m2) of sail—truly a sight to behold. At the time, these cats were the fastest thing on water, but their terrifying speed brought the problem of stress on their wing masts, mainsheet travellers, crossbeams, hulls, and foils.

We saw the famous Tiger Cat that set standards when it won the '78 USA One-of-a-Kind and was the breakthrough that put catamarans on the map. The then fabulous 18 ft. (5 m) Pacific Cat was also competing, and years later I saw one of these sturdy P Cats in Honolulu Yacht Harbour. It had done a single-handed crossing from California and the skipper had all the turnbuckles replaced with line because he did not trust turnbuckles in Pacific conditions! All the cats we had been reading about were suddenly before our eyes, including Aqua Cat, Phoenix, Hobie 14, and A Class Australis all the way from Australia. Trimarans were on the scene, too, including the Piver. A few years later, the designer, Piver, became one of the sailing world's mysteries when he and his boat disappeared from the face of the earth. The Hobie 14 was to become the world's most popular cat, until the Hobie 16 appeared on the scene. This is where I made a life long acquaintanceship with a young Hobie Alter, who was rigging his 14 around the corner from us near the Long Beach Yacht Club.

The on-the-water time trials had us sailing through a measured distance of about 660 ft. (200 m). The wind was around 30 mph. (48 km/h) at sea level, and we went through the trap three times. We placed third fastest overall, which was no mean feat considering the depth of the competition. Around the race course in light winds, we did not fare well. Hans analyzed the matter and believed our planing hulls had too much wetted area, and the drag slowed us down. Also, each wave that hit our bow hit the

A catamaran weekend with Yachting Worlds racing Flying Kittens

Life in the Sailboat World

hull again just aft of mid-ship; this was the reason none of the many planing-hull cats became a consistent success. I know that 19th century naval engineers established that the fastest way to move through the water was with a U-shaped hull, and that the famous Scottish Prout brothers said that every 25 lbs. (11 kg) makes a difference in a catamaran, which was proved right time after time. So, as good as our beloved FK was in heavy winds, sad to say she was doomed; never mind she was so labour intensive to build.

The Long Beach experience taught me sailing without gloves is a no-no. My hands were raw from the salt-impregnated wet sheets (ropes). We found some American made leather Trophy Gloves, which were balm on our hands, and to this day, Glenmore Boats sells this brand, despite the new polyester guys on the block from Harken, Ronstan, Holt Allen, and others.

First Glimpse of the
Sea Spray 15-Foot-Catamaran

At one of the parties the night before the competition, Duuk van Heel, a four time World Champion Flying Junior skipper and now a Glenmore employee, met Allan Arnold, the designer of the new 15 ft. (4.5 m) Sea Spray catamaran. He was very interested in having Duuk campaign the Sea Spray alongside Henk Pons, a well known racer. Duuk was doing fantastically in the race, way ahead of the other cats, including its main competitors, the Hobie 14, Tornado, and Pacific Cat. Then disaster struck when a two-dollar plastic outhaul slide broke. Duuk sailed to a breakwater, nervous about his thin hulls on the rough boulders, but managed with great loss of time to jury rig the system. Although he lost the race, everyone had been alerted to the terrific little single-hander hidden in the 15 ft. (4.5 m) Sea Spray. We told Jack Holt in England about the failure of his outhaul slide, but as usual, we, the customer, were in the wrong: he told us we must have overloaded it.

We had had a previous run-in with Jack Holt when he copied

our FK pivoting, mast-raising casting. He acknowledged the copying and offered us a one penny royalty for future units sold, complaining at the same time that his parts were being copied all over the world. We are still waiting for our royalties.

The world might have been inundated by various sized Sea Sprays instead of Hobies. When we sat next to marketing genius Hobie Alter at the banquet, he spoke very highly of the Sea Spray design and said he may well have gone towards Sea Spray had it been on the scene earlier. He told the designer, Allan Arnold, the same thing, but that's all history, or is it water under the bridge? Hobie became the real champion when he achieved sales of nearly a quarter of a million catamarans.

A Few Sailing Tips

Sailors still ask me for dinghy and cat handling or tuning sessions, and often I think I will have a quiet weekend at the lake, only to find myself out on the water for a coaching session with a new boat owner. I find owners of larger yachts usually need help with weather or lee helm, meaning they have found their boat has a mind of its own, wanting to turn into the wind or off the wind. It seems simple enough when you know it, but teaching the basics in baby language, and working with mast angles and sail settings is often demanding stuff!

I mostly counsel or teach as a courtesy and often get a pleasant week's sailing out of the deal, but sometimes I charge a fee, and in retirement this means a little pocket money. With a light breeze I can, in an afternoon session, often teach a few tricks of the trade that normally come with years of sailing and racing. My idea is to enhance sailing skills and not teach from scratch. My sessions usually include the best type of rigging for the prevailing wind, coming about efficiently, and safe jibing, which is considered by many the most dangerous maneuvre in sailing. A boom can swing across a boat violently, and before you know it, someone has been knocked into the water. I try to teach the best methods of climbing

The Compleat Sailor: PFD, gloves, stopwatch, sun-hat, boots, wetsuit, sunglasses, and sunblock

(going into the wind at about 45 degrees or better), reaching (sailing at a 90-degree angle to the wind), broad reaching, and running (having the wind behind you at a true 180 degrees). I also teach how to approach waves to prevent bow diving and to give extra speed. This means sailing a wavy course and releasing the jib for a split second — anything to avoid coming to a dead stop. It is frightening in heavy winds to see a catamaran dive into the water six feet or more or even do a complete cartwheel. I have seen dinghies dive so violently that mast failure occurred. The most important aspect I try to get across is where the wind is coming from and acting accordingly. Besides a wind indicator, one must look for different water colours, the wind on one's cheeks and on the hair on one's hands, together with slight tremors in the sails.

Upside Down in the Atlantic

In 1971, Gen Mar Inc., the American Sea Spray builder, asked me to represent them, all expenses paid, in a major multihull regatta at Rowayton, Connecticut. They saw my winning many races as good enough credentials. Upon arrival at the Rowayton Club, I found a great many Aqua Cats on the scene and was told that the Hobie 14 would be introduced. I felt the pressure of having to give a winning Sea Spray performance after the grueling trip to get me and a boat there; Calgary suddenly seemed a long way away.

I flew into La Guardia, New York, about 10:00 p.m. and met our Toronto Sea Spray dealer, Pat McGrath, who brought the boat. He was bushed from a rough trip and insisted I drive through the night to Connecticut via New York's nightmare traffic. To add to the angst, Air Canada had lost my suitcases containing my vital sails and foils. In those days, they were good at finding luggage, and we were relieved when a taxi delivered the cases to our motel the next morning.

Pat and I had arrived at the motel in the middle of the night and immediately started filling the gudgeon holes with resin so they could be redrilled in the morning. Our aim was to cut down play in the rudders for more speed, and it worked like a charm! We worked away in our motel room with resin, hardener, putty, and tools. We even ironed the sails to remove the creases. With visions of all those Aqua Cats out there, we had to use all the tricks; racers should note that using a damp towel to iron is a good tip. Over the years I saw factory boats built especially for competition, with gossamer lay-ups, no foam, light masts, special sails, and extra fared and polished foils. I always thought this unfair competition, and certainly the Sea Spray we used was no more than average and even a little long in the tooth.

Life in the Sailboat World

On the first race day, I had an average start, but sailed through a myriad of Aqua Cats to be first at the weather pin and never saw the other boats again. I was able to repeat this in the remaining races that day. On the second day, the local radio announced a small craft warning, in Long Island Sound, and the news was posted at the Rowayton Yacht Club. At the skippers' meeting, we were told we were going out at our own risk, and in view of all the expense and effort to get me there, I decided to race: the show had to go on. Already, in the first race, a horrendous wind blew in. The mainsail of a Tornado cat just ahead shredded, and it capsized. I learned later that the winds were 90 mph. (145 km/h) and were rated at light hurricane.

I capsized, too, then got my boat up, but it blew right over again. I sensed that water had entered my mast and once three feet (one metre) of water has entered a mast, it is just about impossible to right a boat. I always recommend sealing masts and checking often for bubbles by holding below water level. The counter-weight of water in a mast about 22 feet (7 metres) away from the sailor is unmanageable. Masts left our factory sealed, but rivets work loose, and nothing would have made much difference under those howling conditions. Some builders insert foam sticks in the mast, which works if the internal halyards are not impeded, but here again, the foam can take on moisture and create another set of problems. Nowadays, there are large airfoil shaped polyethylene buoyancy devices for the top of the mast.

I sat on my inverted hull, back to the wind, and my Helly Hansen oilskins absolutely protected me from wind chill and hypothermia. Glenmore sold those original yellow Norwegian oil skins, starting in the early seventies, and I still believe that with all the advances in wet gear, the Hellys measure up to anything. I find it hard to believe now, but I drifted for five hours, all the time thinking that if I wanted to survive, I had better stay cool and calm. Out of the hazy fog came an Islander 32 yacht asking if I wanted a tow. Still trying to act calmly, I accepted with much appreciation and relief. I told "Islander" my mast was down and the sails were still rigged. The skipper threw me cable cutters, warning me the Continental Shelf was a few miles offshore and would ruin the mast. I cut the forestay, and the whole rig floated horizontally aft under the trampoline once we were underway. We arrived at a protected cove where the Islander owner had a mooring, and we pulled the Sea Spray on shore away from the wind and the wash.

"Mrs. Islander" could see I was cold and needed food, but first made me a Scotch in a milk shaker, the best Scotch I've ever had to this day. They hydrated me and topped it up with Mexican salad, and contentment set in. Suddenly, we heard a loud motor boat and were hailed by a Rowayton Yacht Club crew looking for a blue Sea Spray. I thanked my Islander rescuers and stayed in touch with them for some twenty years. The searchers towed me back to Rowayton at breakneck speed, and I grimly hung on to my tiller to keep the rudders at 90 degrees, knowing I could easily catapult. It was actually the most frightening part of my hurricane capsize in Long Island Sound.

As a result of my first day's successes, AMF-Alcort ordered 700 Sea Sprays from Gen Mar Inc. and named them Sea Moth. It was identical to the Sea Spray, except for the name and insignia.

I feel no sailor should go out when there is a small craft warning or if a black ball is hung. I have noticed time and time again that regatta organizers simply don't have enough rescue boats for emergencies. When the wind gods dish it out, be prepared to sit it out on an inverted boat, often on a sparsely populated shoreline. Never mind how benign the weather, carry on board water, power bars, and sun block. If the weather looks iffy, a shorty wet suit is not too cumbersome and prevents the vital trunk area from losing warmth. A true sou'wester prevents heat loss and gives amazing front and back protection. Non-slip footwear is vital on the boat, as well, for protection on rough shore landings.

My personal choice has been Harken shoes or Gill booties, and knee boots can be good, too. The federal requirements of 50 feet

(15.24 m) of floating throw line, paddle, bailer, and whistle, along with an approved PFD are all life savers. Make sure your young children have PFDs with crotch straps.

The Sailing Game

Life in the Sailboat World

Chapter 2

Sailboat Business Beginnings

The Aqua Cat

Larry Bacon of Newport Beach, then a small sleepy California town, sold the Aqua Cat, which was built by American Sail, Inc. of North Carolina. He thought I should become a Canadian dealer. They were the only other significant cat manufacturer at the time. It is pleasing to note American Sail is still in business, selling a few boats and probably lots of parts for the many thousands of Aqua Cats it sold over the years.

Audrey and I vacationed in Oceanside after the multihull event, and Larry dropped off and rigged an Aqua Cat, which we had fun surf sailing the whole week. The tripod rig was quite effective, and she was reasonably stable, but not as fast as I had expected. Probably due to my inexperience, I broke the dagger-boards, rudders, and gudgeon and tripod castings, driving her through the surf all day. The factory, together with Larry, prompt-ly sent me replacement parts on a daily basis. The service was excellent and beyond the call of duty, but by the end of the week I decided against taking on the dealership.

Not much later, Peter Shuley from Vancouver took her on and made her sound like the fastest eighth world wonder; he sold a lot of Aqua Cats across the country, perhaps as many as 1,500 over 10 years. I always considered him a typical promoter. He worked hard, talked fast, and convinced a lot of Canadians that this was the catamaran for them. As often happened, I felt I was the winner in the long run. The Sea Spray 15 cat, which we started represent-ing in 1968, sailed circles around the Aqua Cat. It was almost like comparing a Chevrolet to a Ferrari. Huge sales came from Aqua

Cat sailors moving up to the much faster, computer designed Sea Spray, and we sold over 2,000 in the ensuing years.

The Sea Spray 15 Catamaran

During the 1968 World Multihull Championship, I had serious discussions with Allan Arnold about his 15 ft. Sea Spray catamaran. My gut was telling me here was something special, and I decided to import one on the double to feel out the market. All the talk in the world doesn't do as good as to see and feel the product.

Allan Arnold's claim to fame was that while working for NASA as an aero-stress engineer, he came up with the successful idea to use fibreglass in the Apollo heat shields, which up to then had been melting on re-entry into the earth's atmosphere. He also designed the fuel tanks for the Saturn rockets and was responsible for farming out contracts worth $1 billion. Allan was born in England and had come to Canada to work on the Avro Arrow fighter plane. He was one of the 10,000 aeronautical engineers who lost their jobs when the Diefenbaker government scrapped the Avro contract. These highly skilled engineers drifted into the space industry and, while Allan was at North American Aviation, he computer designed the Sea Spray and tested it in the wind tunnels. He was able to design strength into this craft, which enabled it to be built at unheard of light weight. The sails, originally including a sock main, had an area of 125 sq. ft. (90 in main and 35 jib — 11.61 m2). No wonder it was fast! It was deemed a single-hander, but was well able to be sailed by two if they were not monsters.

The sample Sea Spray arrived, and we invited sailors from the two major yacht clubs to try her on Calgary's Glenmore Reservoir. They could not believe her light weight, finger tip control and speed, and the only criticism concerned the sock sail, which meant the mast could only be raised after the sock had been threaded on it. This was not easy when launching from a dock. Despite this, we sold twelve the first week at an introductory price of $1,199 Cdn

An early North American Sea Spray championship with 51 entries

and solved the sock sail problem by offering a halyard version. This made her even more popular. At the same time, we were competing with the new one-man Laser, which also had a sock sail and an even heavier two-piece mast, selling at an introductory $799 Can. Most folks don't remember the price was increased to $1,000 Cdn pretty quickly, and that the $799 deal was only a Quebec price for factory seconds.

Glenmore Boats was now in its infancy, utilizing the battery company's employee, Marvin Twain (yet another story) and, on a part time basis, my sailing partner, Hans Kreuz.

We needed an extrusion for the Sea Spray's new halyard sail and designed a light weight PVC sleeve to rivet onto the aluminum mast. We sealed its multiple rivets by swiveling gunk inside the 20 ft. (6.09 m) long tube. Taylor Sails of Montana redesigned the early sock pattern into a classic bolt rope main, and

Life in the Sailboat World

**80 mph (130 km/h) Chinook winds decimate the championship.
Jim Peyto has already broken his mast.**

although we lost some sail area doing this, we learned early the sailor does the dictating in the market place.

The trials of starting a new company in a field we knew little about were just about to begin! The first 20 suits of sails we brought in from Windward Sails in England had to be shipped back twice for non-compliance with specifications and instructions. We quickly learned that mistakes are mostly somebody else's fault and very costly, and that the extra costs always landed on our doorstep.

The presold 12 Sea Sprays arrived from Allan Arnold. Talk about a fiasco! They all took on water, from dribbles to near sinkings. We had to pacify a good few irate sailors and we soon became very proficient in detecting leaks with stethoscopes and vacuums in true Rube Goldberg fashion. We made a million phone calls to Allan Arnold, seeking guidance, and while he always tried to be helpful, we did not really solve the numerous failures we were enduring. In a nutshell, these troubles were coming from poor workmanship. Allan was working in a garage, like so many of the early boat builders, including Sunfish and Hobie. Even though the California temperatures and humidity were near perfect for fibreglassing, the men were piece workers, and there was no chance for quality control while working on a shoestring.

These problems lay heavily on us, along with the impractical sock sail and long supply line, so we decided to start up production in Calgary. We had to take destiny in our hands as we did with the Flying Kitten. We bought a set of Sea Spray plugs from Allan Arnold, from which we could make molds, and came to a satisfactory arrangement and good friendship with Allan, which lasts to this day. He never stinted on boat building, technical, engineering, and aeronautical advice. We in turn registered the design in Ottawa and paid Allan a royalty for each Sea Spray we sold in the following ten years. Following tradition, we started manufacturing in garage space, which served us well for fifteen years

The growth phenomenon of Sea Spray in Canada was nothing short of spectacular as these figures show:

1968/69 — 25 sold
1970 — 75 sold
1971 — 110 sold
1972 — 150 sold

At the first 1971 North American Sea Spray Championship in Calgary, there were 38 Sea Sprays at the start, including a lot of Americans, which was a phenomenal number for a new class. The occasion was memorable in more ways than one when, after fair winds, an 80 mph. (128.75 km/hr.) Chinook wind blew in and capsized just about the whole fleet; a lot of damage occurred, and a few people were in shock. Glenmore Boats had a service unit on site, and we got virtually all the "destruction derby" boats back on the water for the following day's races. The City of Calgary rescue-boat team was in its infancy, but it got a lot of practice that day.

Hans Kreuz took the championship and regained it three times over the next decade. In fact, Canadians kept the North American cup for the next 24 years, except once, when Tom Storey of San Francisco Bay took it. Outstanding victors over the years were Duuk van Heel, Hans Kreuz, and Barry Lester—four times, Paul Stenning, Dave West—eleven times, Stan Storwick, Roy Smith, and Americans Jay Gardner, Tom Storey, and Robbie Harvey.

These results are surprising, considering Canadians have to be content with a very short sailing/training season of perhaps four months, enduring ice, snow, and frost the rest of the time. On top of that, Canadians generally sail on liquid ice and only in high summer would you want to fall in the water. Wet or dry suits are a must and often provide the thin line between fun and tragedy.

Sea Spray Growing Pains

The growth of the Sea Spray did not go unnoticed, and a long established builder in Calgary, Smallcraft of Canada, saw fit to copy her, first calling it the Playmate, then Playcat, and last but not least, Firecat. Initially, they took some sales away, but were soon having problems with their spars, sails, and crossbeams. They had basically followed the design of our registered patent, and we were advised we stood a good chance of stopping those rascals from proceeding any further. Indeed, the judge told them to stop whatever they were doing and to pay the court costs.

Having to pay these court costs and the failure of a $50,000 loan negotiation put them into bankruptcy. We shed no tears, and in later years, for all its misgivings, Glenmore benefited greatly from servicing the many sailboats Smallcraft had sold in its time. We bought the Enterprise and SC18 molds from the bankruptcy trustee and also considered the Fireball and Flying Junior molds. The latter was very difficult to build in fibreglass within class rules, having been originally designed to be made out of wood

A boat is only as good as its mold-girls polish her with loving attention

with sharp 90-degree angles. The rolling out of resin in those areas is very difficult and time consuming, and builders often employed female laminators who seem to have more aptitude for the careful work needed to keep blisters out. In hindsight, we should have taken on the Flying Junior and Fireball, which remain popular; the few manufacturers left want a lot of money.

The well known international sailor, Duuk van Heel, had been working at Smallcraft and now joined Glenmore. He agreed to stay for two years, then intended to return to The Netherlands to join his generations-old family business in banking and commodity trading. Both he and Hans Kreuz made inestimable contributions to Glenmore.

Our company was in its first strong growth pattern. In 1970, I had made a deal with Hans Kreuz to take charge of the commercial production of the Sea Spray catamaran. His work involved purchasing the standing and running rigging, acres of aluminum for masts, booms, rudders, daggerboards, ropes, and sails; not to mention the fastenings, fittings, and backing plates. A major innovation in 1980 was to make the hulls of Coremat, a "sandwich" material producing unheard of strength, but very light. Up until then, Coremat was only used on high stress areas.

In 1969, we shipped a slatted wooden crate 15 ft. x 2 ft. x 2 ft. (4.57 m x 0.61 m x 0.61 m) containing a Sea Spray destined for Canada's premier International Boat Show, then held each year at Toronto's CNE Automotive Building. We continued to exhibit in Toronto for the next 22 years — an unprecedented record for a boat builder, not to mention one from inland Calgary. As time went by, we added other models to our display, but in 1990 decided against exhibiting, because the 7% GST had arrived, and we felt that sales would be affected. Looking back, it was a wise decision, or shall we say, intuition. The Gulf War had started, and that year there was a blinding snowstorm in greater Toronto. Torontonians can take a lot, but they don't like driving in snowstorms, and the show was a disaster. In fact, we started having such profitable years from western business, we decided to stop exhibiting in Toronto. Instead, we became visitors to the notable Toronto International Boat Show, acquiring many new products and absorbing new trends, which led business in Calgary to progress even faster. I am not sure what the moral of this strange situation was, but it was all good!

It was easy to ship a disassembled Sea Spray in a slatted wooden crate. We cut the mast in two at the 5 ft. (1.52 m) mark and it easily rejoined with a stuffer block. To reassemble the cat took about an hour. We shipped Sea Sprays in this easy manner throughout the seventies and eighties. When Duuk van Heel left us in 1974, he took a Sea Spray back to Holland and entered her in the first ever Round Texel Island Race, a grueling course with horrendous tides and currents. It proved a difficult race for any small cat fighting heavy winds and bad chop from shallow waters. In his inimitable style, he placed second out of some 200 cats, but a Hobie 14 from Berlin beat him. To this day, I don't understand how the great Duuk was beaten by an even shorter hulled catamaran with 10% less sail. It was a great achievement, nevertheless, for the Hobie 14; I must admit, I was once beaten by a Hobie 14 on straight time in light weather near Edmonton. In heavy weather, the 14 benefits from the wider stance of the hulls and her fully battened main. In very light weather, its main is also devilishly efficient. The Sea Spray seems to excel between 2 mph. and 19 mph. (3 km/h and 30 km/h).

In the early years of exhibiting in the Toronto Show, I could always call for help from people like Jos Boelrijk, Pat McGrath, and Bernie Luttmer. I remember one horror story when I lost control stepping a mast surrounded by all kinds of shiny show boats. The mast managed to crash down between two large yachts, but neither mast nor boats were damaged. I remember coping with a fellow rigging a Soling next to me. He was madly swinging his boom back and forth, trying to pop a batten the other way. Cling, cling, cling went my mast, and only after a polite request did it occur to this world class racer to stop the banging—but not without a dirty look.

Selling success continued in Ontario, and Jos Boelrijk of Silent Sports ordered Sea Sprays five at a time, but these orders grew from initial joy into a vicious nightmare. In early summer 1970, a disturbing call came from Boelrijk, informing us some mast crossbeams were buckling. After the first failures, more followed, and we could not figure out the problem. We had ordered all the aluminum to the designer's T6055 specifications (a high strength aircraft type aluminum). We went back to Allan Arnold, the designer, who told us there had never been such an occurrence, even in the heavy seas off the California coast. Alcan was the aluminum supplier, but they refused to do anything unless we could prove their product did not meet specifications. They also politely informed us that even if we did supply proof, Canadian law provides that a manufacturer only has to replace the faulty components. One must sue the manufacturer for product failure, human injury, or death. But, worst of all, there was no way to cover the damage we were to endure in Canada's largest market, southern Ontario. Obviously, we were naive at that point. We were really crushed when Boelrijk told us he would never order another boat.

Life in the Sailboat World

The situation was so serious, we engaged independent engineers (Hardy & Co) to test the cross beams. Indeed, they proved that the wrong aluminum had been supplied. Months went by, however, before Alcan supplied the proper material free of charge. The short Canadian summer had passed, and so had our goodwill and reputation. How consumerism has changed; we should have got hold of a Ralph Nader and made a very loud noise.

Our main competition, Hobie, ran away with the ball as a result of the Ontario Sea Spray fiasco, and we never overcame the blow dealt us by Alcan. Sure, we sold a Sea Spray here and there, but nothing like the huge market that developed in Western Canada.

It was not all bad news, though, and we had our first ever National Championship on Chestermere Lake, hosted by the venerable Calgary Yacht Club, around since 1934. We were honoured

The company moves into cruising sailboats

Life in the Sailboat World

that they agreed to hold a catamaran event after a long history of monohull fleets, such as Lake Sailers, Y-Flyers, and Enterprises. Hans Kreuz's coaching paid off, and I took this first ever Nationals, only to loose my crown next year to Jim Peyto of Banff.

Reputation travels and stays with you. I met Jim Peyto on Lake Windermere in British Columbia where he sailed the traditional 2-man Snipe. After seeing the Sea Spray cat in action and because he never could find crew for the Snipe, he bought a Sea Spray. I took some time showing him the subtleties of cat sailing; he was another one of those natural sailors and, as mentioned, promptly beat me in the 1970 championship. He was also a natural pilot and a few years later, we were shocked when he killed himself hitting wires during an emergency landing.

As a matter of interest a National Championship places sixth in the order of importance in the racing venues which range as follows: Fleet, Club, City, Provincial, Regional, National, North American, World, Olympic Games.

Years of Stunning Growth 1973-79

This was a time when it would be nothing to sell 25 boats a day and came about when we expanded into a second boat, the 12 ft. Kolibri, which hailed from Atlanta Bootsbau of south Germany.

Electrical Engineer Klaus Schneeberger, the owner and president, had invented injection-molding mass production, which was a way to make a well equipped sailboat at a low price. The hull and deck were bonded together with glue and steam heat after foam sheets and contoured floatation were placed inside the hull. She was unsinkable.

Klaus manufactured many of the components in his huge, 700-employee German factory and he became world competitive. He had assembly plants in Japan, Brazil, South Africa, Australia, and two each in Canada and the US. He approached us in 1972 to take on Kolibri assembly, where we could make seven boats a day with two good men.

Our magnificent Airdrie plant produced the Sea Spray , the DS 16, the Enterprise, the Commodore 15, and the Kolibri 2-12

The project scared the hell out of us when we accepted the deal. We would receive the first container with 50 disassembled hulls and decks, foam, sails, spars, hardware, etc., along with a second container with 15 ft. metal steam-assembly jigs and piping, and additional woodwork for the boats. Glenmore had to acquire the steam making machine. Klaus was to come to teach the assembly, and $50,000 had to be paid prior to the containers leaving Germany. This was big money for us, but after the first transaction, he allowed us to pay for 90-boat containers after the boats were sold. This generally meant three months credit, but we had no trouble extending to eight months without interest, if needed. The arrangement gave us exclusivity in the four western provinces. Skene Boats of Ottawa had the eastern Canadian rights.

Assembly went well with only minor problems, like pintles and rudderheads breaking, failing turnbuckles, and warped foils.

But there was another headache; all the floatation in one 90-boat container took on moisture coming through the Panama Canal, and the foam got so swollen, it wouldn't fit inside the Kolibri. Atlanta Bootsbau air-shipped replacement foam in days, no questions asked. Atlanta was a fine example of the handshake era.

Socially, we got close to Klaus, as well as finding him top notch on the business front; he had no tricks up his sleeve. We thought it important to maintain good relations with just about all our suppliers, and mourn the current lack of ethics, openness, and niceties. Klaus told us that selling boats all over the world

Intricate deck bonding

Life in the Sailboat World

involved him in high finance, and he often had to pay 45% interest on short term money to keep his German bankers happy.

Thanks to brainy sailors on board like Hans Kreuz and Duuk van Heel, we quickly solved any manufacturing trouble spots and managed to get the massive 15 ft. long steam assembly jigs up and running prior to Klaus' first visit. We were anxious to get pre-sold Kolibris out the door.

We had another great shock when we learned in January 1976 that Klaus had hit tree tops in Munich in low cloud when landing his twin engine Dornier, coming back from the London Boat Show. Klaus was an expert pilot with 9,000 hours under his belt. Two other executives were killed, and Atlanta Bootsbau was destroyed within a year. Seven hundred people lost jobs in a one industry town, and the world lost an innovative boat builder; his stable of Kolibri, Koralle, 17 ft. Daysailer, and fishing boats came to an end.

We had been selling container loads of Kolibris, and there was still a huge demand. For a while, we turned away business, but then started to make our own version, calling her Kolibri 2-12. The Kolibri 2-12 became a major product in our sailboat line, reaching into the 21st century.

Walk Out

Sometime in late 1978, my production manager and his assistant gave notice. We replaced these two valuable players, after a considerable search, with Jim Gingrich who had a fibreglass shop which had run into some product trouble. He was a bright person and caught on fast to what was involved in boat building. I believe our operations took a big step forward under his professional supervision; he insisted on total independence in all facets of the production personnel and purchasing.

Within a year, he requested a new plant; he felt our operations had outgrown the existing modest premises. Indeed, our production had risen substantially, and we looked for a new home. The only reasonable land was in Airdrie, 19 miles (30.57 km) north of Calgary, and financing was arranged through the Alberta Opportunity Company. A 10,000 sq. ft. (929 m2) steel plant was built rapidly with such amenities as 30-second continuous air replacement and showers for workers to prevent fibreglass itch. Financially, we were in quite deep, and I think my gut felt warning signals, despite our advisors' insistence that our capital investment in land, plant, and equipment was nothing short of brilliant.

There was suddenly a strong need to acquire more sales and dealers to consume a production line steadily pumping out Sea Sprays, Kolibris, DS16s, SC18s, Commodores, and Enterprises. I wanted to take on outside fibreglass contracts and build a wider sales base, but Gingrich protested he was hired to build boats, and if we wanted it differently, he would quit. We did not find this an empty threat, having determined after advertising all over the country that there were no fibreglass production managers to be had.

By then, his wife was doing an excellent job as plant administrator, and pretty soon we saw his teen children filling plant jobs. I encouraged Gingrich to sail with me to learn how theory worked in practice; after a short period, he claimed he knew it all. Within a year he bought a Sea Spray cat for his son and a 25 ft. Tanzer yacht for himself, all at cost plus 5%.

By now, we had about 25 people at the plant. It was very difficult to get good workers as the oil market was on another high, paying absurd wages. We were forced to pay our lowest factory worker management rates, and they didn't even have to guarantee the bank loans! Something was out of kilter, and I could smell the economy faltering.

I took a ten-day trip into the Pacific Northwest, attempting to set up dealers in Montana, Idaho, and Washington, my Jeep pulling a tandem trailer laden with sample products. The grades in the Rockies were a great trial, but I could see the dealers were overstocked with non-selling products. I remember selling a few boats in Missoula, but it was slim pickings. I had to face it—there was another recession upon us.

Our next move was to exhibit at the prestigious Marine Trade Show in Chicago's McCormack Centre. I was familiar with this huge show, having manned a stand for the American Sea Spray manufacturer. After a two-day haul through Saskatchewan, North Dakota, Minnesota, and Illinois, I drove straight into the centre. I was set upon by a group of burly men demanding I get out of the hall. It was the union at work; they had the sole right to unload. I told them that it had been a long haul, but after getting my boats to Chicago undamaged, I begged them to give my boats the same loving care. They did.

Just the same, I found it a dreadful experience, and so, perhaps, did others. Later on, McCormack Center lost this important marine show to a less autocratic union site in Fort Lauderdale, Florida.

We were warned to turn right, leaving McCormack, but like fools went the wrong way and ended up in an African American slum that had Kafka written all over. It was like a bomb site, whole houses eviscerated or in a terrible, dilapidated state, with floors missing, broken windows, and no paint. Children played in the middle of potholed roads, and elders stood by to protect them. We locked the car doors and left quickly, but that devastating sight of poverty lives on in my mind.

Our Chicago experience ended happily, with sizable orders from some 35 dealers across the Midwest, including Twin Cities; now we had to rush home and get the product made and delivered.

I have to say that with all its fame, I found the Chicago show to have a somewhat provincial face. I was approached by many smaller and medium sized firms, but learned at my father's knee that it is better to have a hundred small accounts than two large dealers; their money is the same. I have seen manufacturers get into deep trouble from loosing a major dealer. The presence of the upstart Canadian Glenmore Boats at the show was noted by AMF-Alcort, then a major force in the American small boat industry with their Sunfish. They took predatory action by lowering prices on conflicting models.

The situation became rather murky; Glenmore was the Sunfish dealer in Calgary and knew their price structures. We really sold a lot of their fine Trac catamarans and Sunfishes, so the shock was even greater when AMF closed its doors a couple of years later. We leaped at the chance to buy their entire Seattle warehouse stock at a super low price. Once again, I jumped in my trusty Jeep and brought the 1500 lb. (680.39 kg) load over the Cascade Mountain summits, hardly making 5 mph. (8 km/h).

Audrey Joins Glenmore

For sixteen years, Audrey had done administration in a law firm absorbing lots of management ideas, as well as learning about the law. I had always discussed Glenmore's business with her, but in the seventies we grew like wildfire, and there was a greater need for management. Fast decisions were often needed, and the continual phone discussions were irritating her boss, with reason. She quit to concentrate on Glenmore, but to this day, she and her former employer remain good friends and talk often.

She became a force to be reckoned with. New management systems were instituted and the high standard of office/sales procedures reflected the large company Glenmore had become. It often amazed me in the seventies and eighties how companies got away with sloppy paper work, and I realized business was ripe for the discipline of computerized record keeping. Audrey also had a talent for client communication and became a star salesman. She insisted all employees have deep product knowledge and devised very informative product literature. We kept our business on a cash basis and got no bad cheques in forty years, which is a true test of the calibre of sailors, never mind our management.

We did run into a Puerto Rican customer, who would only pay for eleven of the twelve boats we sent him in a container, claiming this would protect any warranty problems. A novel idea;

we rarely had warranty claims, but always made a point to settle them the same day.

Under an Ottawa sponsored cost sharing deal, we again exhibited in Chicago. We sold well, including the foregoing load of Sea Sprays to Puerto Rico. We undertook to be present when the boats arrived and booked at what we thought was a decent San Juan hotel. The Canadian trade commissioner advised us to quit the hotel, not go in any side streets, and invited us to stay at the

CBC and CTV sent crews to chronicle the new Airdrie plant.

Life in the Sailboat World

consulate. This was only 1980, yet the consulate had three security systems, and one needed to contact the local police upon exiting. The trade commissioner proved a fine host and introduced us to intriguing Caribbean food.

I went to the beach and helped the new dealer assemble the first Sea Spray and demonstrated her through the three-foot surf. You could not walk barefoot on the hot sand, and breaking open the wooden crates in scorching 109° F (42.77° C) heat was plain awful!

We started to believe our own publicity!

Life in the Sailboat World

While walking the streets behind the beach, a truckload of islanders came by yelling "hey whitey—go home" and making cut-throat gestures. No kidding. We were happy being under the protection of the consul and were even happier flying away from the white hot beaches of Puerto Rico.

Audrey claims she learned selling from me; well, if that was the case, she developed her own, more powerful variation. We subtly let customers deal with whom they felt most comfortable, and often one would sell where the other had failed. She had an instinctive feeling about people's desires and zeroed in with a few questions. It fascinated me.

Hundreds of books have been written on how to sell, but I still believe some degree of natural talent is involved and is merely honed on the battlefield. I have seen her time and again sell a boat when others had given up. Soul searing patience has something to do with it. Really, we are all sales people, selling ourselves to partners, bosses, fellow employees, and a stream of daily contacts. It happened often that a client stood totally puzzled as to what they wanted, but walked out with a water toy they had fallen in love with. We sometimes received little gifts or wine from customers who found sailing had enhanced their life. We thought of ourselves more as counselors fitting the right product to the right person.

Audrey, this paragon of virtue, had also a knack of training staff in her image, particularly in the matter of administration. From our early website we developed a mail order business, which expanded worldwide. She designed procedures to control this field, which easily eats profit from inefficiency. While some staff fought management discipline, many told us later that it smoothed the way when they started businesses. I remember her working patiently with a dyslexic boy, but his thanks were somewhat galling when we discovered his hand in the till.

A very smart employee developed our website early in the game, and while it was pretty low key, it generated a huge increase in business. Orders just flowed in while we slept. The business became more demanding, and most of the time we worked 60-plus hours every week and had to take separate holidays. Sad to say, we even missed the funerals of our parents in Europe.

Another part of the job was dealing with the bank, and in the beginning, we were desperate for financing to carry us through seven months of no-income winter. She became adept at these negotiations and a deft hand with projections and spread sheets. Later, a banker told her in confidence that his department used to make bets on the closeness of her projections. Some very bright bankers crossed our path and helped with our chronic shortage of winter working capital by offering a balloon financing scheme. We had rigid annual repayments due in the summer, but in this manner we strengthened the company's base; it was a godsend. However, the banks, being what they were, still demanded all manner of personal collateral, which we did not begrudge; we thought of it as having trust in ourselves. We seemed to get along with all these bankers, and most became valuable clients when they needed water toys.

Dermatomyositis, a strange, rare autoimmune illness overtook Audrey right after the 1988 Olympics. She thought her body was protesting the long stressful hours, saying, if you won't slow down, I will do it for you. At the worse times, she couldn't lift a pound and took about forty minutes just to get out of bed. On top of it all, she turned lobster red! She couldn't work or do much else, but after a year, she began operating from home, keeping a handle on the business and the accounting. It took five long years to rid this scourge from her body, but a brilliant specialist, acres of cortisone, and daily physiotherapy did the trick.

Today she downhill skis, hikes, and bikes for untold hours. We took up leisure kayaking and have had a few wind-strewn lake experiences. Next, we plan to try the Hobie Mirage pedaling kayaks. Our company and private lives mingled, but it seemed to work.

The Sailing Game

Life in the Sailboat World

Chapter 3

Boat Shows

Boat Show Time and Tips

Canadian boat shows generally take place January to March and are a necessary evil or, at least, they used to be. One can look forward to dealing with new rules every year.

The builder or dealer has to pay for expensive show space besides extra advertising, free boats, or other major gifts to the show promoters. A myriad of expenses pop up from nowhere, along with overtime, free passes, and show services at obscene rates. Food in boat shows is at least 50% higher and tastes awful, so we often rented apartments to get decent food and make sand-wiches for the show.

It seems a fact of life that common carriers damage sailboats, so we developed our own trailering systems, and cocooned the boats against the elements. We generally loaded in sub zero tem-peratures and drove over treacherous winter roads thousands of kilometres. In the States, shows start earlier, around September. The boat business is like the clothing business in that it needs lead time to have boats at the dealers in time for the sailing season. Boat shows supposedly give an indication of the units to produce.

The public expects to get very fat discounts by buying at the show, but it is hard to give lower prices with all the extra show expenses. We prayed that volume would soften the blow.

Boat shows are not as important as they used to be as, these days, the public can generally bargain throughout the year for the low, low price they saw at the show. Maybe you can lower your prices year round, but can you stay in business? Boat show sales are needed to create cash flow during the long, dry winter.

Talking to the Toronto Boat Show crowds

Glenmore Sailboats exhibited in about 170 shows between 1969 and 2001, mainly in Canada, but at times in the US and Germany. We believe a few cardinal rules helped ensure our success at shows:

We never had the stand look too prosperous; it tends to frighten people away.

We had the staff create a lot of activity on the stand, even if there were no customers. People don't want to feel they will be pounced upon, just because they are the only people on the stand. If staff is unoccupied, they should be dusting boats, tidying or stamping leaflets — there is always something to do.

Having clean, new product in your display and jamming it together creates the illusion the stand is a market crowded with bargains. For some reason, people don't like being the only ones on the stand, but if they can disappear between the mass of boats,

Life in the Sailboat World

they feel less obvious.

We made it easy to enter our stand by having a million welcoming openings.

Our sales people had to have in depth knowledge of the products as we felt it was the only way to be taken seriously in our quest to sell boats. Don't just put warm bodies on your stand. Glib answers won't do, and neither will staff chitchatting to each other. Your eyes need to be scanning for customers, and while they don't want to be engaged immediately, a simple acknowledgement of their presence really pays off. They will find it easier to approach you with questions if contact has already been made.

We approached with open-ended questions or statements that gave the client a reason to talk. It is fun dreaming up openers. Here are a few:

* Are you a sailor already?
* It's a fine sport away from noise.
* You forget all your troubles trying to make your boat go.
* What boat have you been sailing?
* It's a character building sport when children learn to cope with a boat.
* What boats are you familiar with?
* Will you all sail at the same time; if not perhaps you need a smaller boat.
* This boat is very easy to right, even for 10-year-olds.
* This boat is quite light, and two of you can carry it down the beach.
* The wider the boat and the smaller the sail, the more stability it has.
*We often call this craft our nervous wife's boat, as it's so stable.
* This boat is comfortable because you have something to lean against and you can stick your feet straight out.
* It is possible to cartop this kind of boat, but in the long run most people find a trailer more convenient.

Life in the Sailboat World

* Where are you thinking of sailing this summer?
* Even if you haven't sailed since childhood, it comes
      back quickly.
* If your child really likes it, he can go all the way to
      the Olympics in this boat.
* Will you be sailing from your cottage or are you planning
      to join a club... And so on!

Try and hone in on the character of the person to whom you are talking, and mold your future questions to his level of understanding.

Especially in large and out-of-town shows, we made sure the client knew he was on Glenmore's stand. A person walking around a show forgets where he was the minute he comes off the stand and he will probably lose or throw away any card you hand out. He needs a memory jogger, something as simple as pointing to the company sign (make sure he looks too) and asking if he is familiar with the company. We would ask if he had been to our store and describe a nearby landmark. We emphasized that we could deliver anywhere.

We never over or under dressed; conservative, sporty attire or company shirts are ideal. And we never forgot it is the parents or grandparents that sign the cheques. This group is uneasy in the company of long hair, punk, beards, and dirty shoes, and most of us are repulsed by the smell of drink, garlic, onions, and smoke

We always gave our staff 15-minute coffee and 60-minute meal breaks. We recommended they get away from the stand to refresh their spirit, and never let anyone eat on the stand — it is just the wrong image.

We walked the show floor every day just after opening. You must familiarize yourself with what else is going on, so you can immediately take counter steps to not be caught off guard.

We kept a good mix of experienced sales staff of older and younger ages. It is our experience that older buyers have a perception that younger people cannot know the product in depth and are too far away from the management level. You can always call in a young salesperson to give some razzmatazz if there are kids on site. At the other end of the game, young people often give the sales message better, but when the hard bargaining starts, they often need to call in more experienced staff. Sometimes young people are glib because they don't want the client to think they are unknowledgeable. We always impressed on our young staff never to give information they couldn't back up on a witness stand. A simple "I will find out for you" does the job.

We gave our staff a small notebook to take client names and phone numbers, especially if information has been promised. We made sure staff followed up on these leads, because clients find it very impressive that the salesperson was not just blowing hot air when they spoke.

We found it very good to have a daily short sales meeting before opening time. Management has everything in their heads, but needs to remind staff about special offers and other highlights. All our staff had a card stuffed in their pocket with prices for all the boats the company sells. A salesman looks silly if he can't give a price immediately. If a client is honing in on a certain boat, call in your specialist on that product so the best possible knowledge is imparted.

With all good intentions, keep in the back of your head you are there to sell, but to sell the boat that fits the client's lifestyle.

We have refrained from putting staff on commission, because it didn't work for us. It creates tension between staff and with management. Management is often the better salesman, but it quickly annoys staff when they see you honing in on their commission. The public seems to sense commission salesman, and the integrity of the salesperson is lost. We felt staff should be motivated sufficiently with their salaries, and if the company had a good year, we made sure they got Christmas bonuses.

We priced everything on the stand. Some say they don't want competition to know their pricing, but believe me, you will be shopped very early in the game. There is nothing more frustrating than to see a boat that appeals to you and have no idea of the price.

Often a boat turns out cheaper than imagined; we are convinced that price cards sell boats. Ours also included the boat highlights and specs (which the salesperson could secretly peek at too). It is very important to have your company name, address, phone, and email information on the price card; people wander around shows after hours and an informative show card is a silent salesman.

We hung a brochure on each boat; it was surprising how many people I came upon reading this leaflet; and it was a good opening ploy to offer the person a leaflet they could take away. But leaflets cost money; hide them away and only offer one to somebody in whom you have invested time. On the other hand, never be stingy when someone asks for a leaflet.

Here are some of the highlights we emphasized which we know sold product. You might say we were educating the public, but we were really teaching them how to compare the other boats in the show so they could see ours were superior.

The sandwich Coremat construction was so strong you could jump on it, and so we put a sample on the floor and start jumping on it. Then we banged the deck loudly or pushed our knee in the hull to show it didn't indent like many other boats.

You could shave in our shine and that extremely high gloss gelcoat finish was a sign of top notch fibreglassing.

Our anodized masts were twice as strong as any other mast at the show.

We never used run of the mill sails—only top quality North were good enough for our boats.

We emphasized the advantages of single cockpit floors as opposed to double floors, which can delaminate, are not supported evenly, and take on moisture, which freezes and expands in the winter.

We made the jib and mainsheets different colours so that new sailors would instinctively grab the right line in an emergency.

We only used laminated mahogany, not plywood.

Where we could use a superior name fitting we did, such as Harken.

We offered a two-year warranty on the entire craft, but because of our hull strength, could have offered five. The only exclusion were sails, which can be ruined by being left to flap at the dock.

We had attractive colour brochures that contained hard information, as well as specifications. It is enormously helpful for the leaflet to show the boat on a trailer, or being cartopped, or with its spinnaker up, or with the maximum crew it held, or sailing at high speed or just lazing along. These specific views sell boats!

We made it a habit to arrive early to dust our products and vacuum the carpet. We believed in carpet, which dresses up the stand and is a lot easier on the back and legs when standing twelve hours daily.

However good a salesman you are, we avoided falling into the trap of overselling. It does not pay to spend too much time with a prospect, because an unwanted familiarity sets in. Ten to fifteen minutes is more than enough. You are not there to show how much you know, and you can easily confuse a client with too much technical detail. Our approach was to sell the craft on its beauty, attractive price and the major highlights that the client was looking for.

It is a smart idea to give a few minutes to your terms of business so there are no arguments down the road. Our brief message was a 10% to 20% deposit, which could be paid by card, and the balance at the time of shipping in cash or certified funds, but no cards. We also made a point of warning that deposits were non-refundable, and that we wanted them to be sure about the purchase before committing to the sale. Surprisingly, this often firmed their resolve to buy.

Of undeniable help during the boat show years has been jotting down the prospect's name and phone along with an identifier like "red hair." Using their name when they come back, or even months later in the store, is a major psychological victory. There is nothing wrong with asking an interested possible buyer if he minds if you call him in a few days. Tell a good prospect what other goodies he can buy for the boat, and you can often clinch a deal by throwing in a few things or making them half price. Don't give it all away; give the client the pleasure of doing some more bargaining with you, perhaps on the floor model. The sale clincher might also be half price or free delivery to a major point near where they live.

Never neglect eye contact. Lock in the minute you or they talk, and don't allow yourself to be distracted from 100% attention. If you do have to turn away for a second, apologize. Remember you could be laying the basis for a sale years hence.

There was hardly a show where we sold nothing, and even then, sales would always come later. On average we sold from 5 to 20 boats per show, and there was sometimes the thrill of selling up to 70 units, generally to dealers.

It actually does not matter what you sell on the floor, even though it is nice to go home with some cash flow. What does matter is how many contacts you make, spreading the gospel, and giving mental injections about that perfect family boat or cottage dinghy, or that adrenalin-pumping fast catamaran. I often see on other stands staff not starting on time, talking to each other, slouching lazily, and looking demoralized. In fact, within reason, I do not think staff should be sitting while on the stand.

I remember a Toronto competitor accusing us of making tanks because our hulls were so strong. To prove his point, when it was busy, I would climb on the foredeck of our 15 ft. (4.57 m) Commodore and jump up and down, making a hell of a racket; everyone could see there was no creaking or cracking. My competitor across the aisle cringed, as he could not equal this demonstration with his light weight Albacores. The end of this vignette was that we sold many Commodores in Toronto.

We were close-lipped with other exhibitors about our sales, offering modestly that we were moving a few units. The result of boasting is that you often get competitors slashing prices. We felt 10% to 15% deposits were good enough. Anything lower and a client could walk away too easily; anything too high made people nervous with all the bankruptcies around. Deposits are non-refundable by law, but our policy was to hold them over for a year. Many people don't realize their deposit is gone unless it was marked "refundable" in the original contract.

Attending the Toronto show cost us, on average, $10,000 and took us some twenty days. Business was going well just from western sales, so after 1990 we stayed out of Toronto. I have to admit the Department of National Defence (DND) years later gave us huge orders for our Kolibri 2-12, which emanated from repeatedly talking to their officers at the show. When the orders finally came, we shipped our Kolibri to bases from coast to coast, but not without the rigors of building, which we will come to later.

Getting to the Show on Time

Ringing in the New Year meant only one thing for me—leaving for the Toronto Boat Show with the display boats. This was a 4,000 km (2,500 mile) drive each way. I did it for 21 years and sometimes went to the Vancouver Show, too, through the jaws of winter. Such trips usually involved drama of one kind or another and were no mean feat.

Arriving in Toronto, my first task was a huge steam cleaning job to remove road salt. Later we cocooned product and arrived spick and span and shiny. Cartonizing and shrink-wrap was still to come.

Any attempt to ship boats by road or rail always ended with mind-boggling damage and loss of time making the claims. The forwarders never grasped that one can't toss a sailboat around like a package. Probably the highlight of these freight heartbreaks was when a call came from Winnipeg CPR asking if we liked fried sailboats. It soon dawned on me that a dozen crated Sea Spray catamarans had burned in a rail car. CPR wondered if I wanted the smoke blackened shrouds.

Freight loss used to be reimbursed at invoiced sale price, but later, carriers realized their rough handling cost them plenty and

A load of boats being readied for delivery in winter

Life in the Sailboat World

would only pay out our cost. No account was taken of lost time, reshipping, finding proof of value, never mind receivables delay and loss of profit. Now, carriers demand you check goods on arrival, and if no damage is noted, you will probably never make a successful claim. We became experts in receiving goods, reporting and taking photos of damage, and doing all the paper work at delivery time. In the long run, it was an unrewarding waste of time and frustration.

This prompted us to do our own deliveries, and we built large multi-boat trailers and multi-roof racks, all hauled by Jeep trucks.

My new truck driving career was not without close calls, including a 720-degree turn the split second after a semi had passed; I came to a stop at the edge of a cliff. Between Hope and Princeton in freezing snowy weather with a black lake far below, a 21 ft. (6.40 m) cruiser came off my trailer hitch. The safety chain held and an angel in the form of a truck driver stopped to help me hook up again.

I maintain that however careful one is with trailers and pulling vehicles, trouble is always lurking round the corner; I did not want the good luck gods to claim I flirted with them once too often. The Vancouver Boat Show was in a decline and we used this excuse to bow out, but I really think the good luck factor had something to do with it.

The annual trip to Toronto was providing more than enough adventure; I allowed 5 days averaging 800 km (500 miles) a day through ice, frozen rain, and walls of snow. I dived into blizzards east of Regina and emerged north of Toronto. In early days, we did not think to stop and let the front move through. In our angst we kept going, worrying about getting there in time for the show opening.

I remember -105° F (-76° C) wind chill in Saskatchewan when my fibreglass boats chirped like birds as they contracted in the severe temperature. And some motel rooms never warmed up. To alleviate the severe affect the cold had on the Jeep and trailer, I slowed down to 30 to 45 mph. (50 to 70 km/h). In North Dakota I saw hundreds of dead white rabbits strewn over the road, the warmth of the sun on the blacktop being their last hope for survival.

Peering into a howling snowstorm hour after hour gave terrific eye strain, and often, there were no other vehicles for hours on end. I disciplined myself to sit behind the wheel for 12 to 18 hours, always starting with a hearty breakfast. I had lots of liquid aboard and fruit for lunch. At dinner, I let loose and prowled for places that served steak or chicken with wine, and let the day's tensions ease away.

This annual jaunt was not all bad. The incredible natural beauty inspired me, even in the heart of winter. How can one describe the north shore of Lake Superior, except to say a thousand Group of Seven paintings came to life. Dark grey rocks, deep blue-black lakes, and never-ending snow under low overcast skies besotted my senses hour after hour, not to mention the hypnotic feel of endless trees on a lost planet.

I hardly noticed the bad roads between Dryden, Sudbury, Schreiber, Wawa, Spanish River, and Ignace — names engraved on my mind forever like famous battles. Many roads were unpaved, just earth with potholes and washboard, continually menacing my load. One Sunday in -30° F ($-34.44\ ^{\circ}$ C) my alternator failed, and I drove hundreds of kilometres without lights or heater. Having winter emergency clothing onboard prevented me freezing to death. Reaching Winnipeg, I dumped the Jeep for repair and tucked into some steak and eggs at a local eatery.

The magnificent sunsets in Manitoba surely compensated for the bumpy cadenza 62 mi. (100 km) west of Winnipeg. Saskatchewan's endless horizons, in both summer and winter, enchanted me and I could never understand why some found them boring.

The Chinook winds in Alberta and southwest Saskatchewan were a great challenge. They lowered your speed indicator as fast as the gas tank, and often we could not get over 35 mph. (55 km/h).

Life in the Sailboat World

Our little truck could deliver a lot of sailboats

If there has to be a prize for the most fabulous highways, British Columbia would surely be the winner. Enrich your spirit, heart, and eyes in the Fraser Canyon, the Roger's Pass, the Coquilhalla, and the incredible Creston-Salmo, on which a friend told me she felt close to God. These magic highways, with their seasonal moods, do their best to make you scenic drunk or freeze you to the seat with fear as you are buffeted by howling winds on frozen decks.

Somehow my soul absorbed the highway dramas and gave me the will to fight upcoming battles in yet another boat show. We had to face a hundred zany comments as to what happens when the bed sheets (sails) come down, what is the high stick (mast) for, you-don't-speak-French-go-to-hell, it's great to see a Calgary firm here!

Conclusions About Boat Shows

The basic problem is that floor space has become unrealistically expensive at $4.00 to $8.00 per square foot; a company has to sell a lot of product to gain back that kind of expense. The show promoters, such as CNE in Toronto, Stampede Board in Calgary, PNE in Vancouver, and Northlands Coliseum in Edmonton, have shown a pattern, in my opinion, of losing touch with the needs of their exhibitors. Often, we felt there was insufficient local advertising to support the shows, and the boating industry began to show resistance to exhibiting. Management, in turn, has brought in many non-marine displays to fill up the space, and we began seeing wall climbing, dog and pig races, trout pools, credit card sellers, bicycle performers, and orthotic shoe sellers, to name only a few. The special sanctity of visiting the annual boat show began to evaporate and along with it the well-heeled buyers.

This uneasy relationship has seen boat dealers in many areas set up independent shows exclusively dedicated to boats. We saw it first in Winnipeg in the early eighties, where the marine sector profitably organized their own show with decreased floor space costs. The premier Toronto Show sold out to an American group as a result of financial problems. Calgary boat dealers had flirted successfully with a few minor shows; then in 2001, the dealers organized a splendid boats-only show in the just finished Telus Convention Centre—lots of windows, ample lighting and carpeting, very consumer friendly. There was heavy local advertising, with exhibitors paying lower space costs and receiving rebates from the profits. Glenmore certainly had its best show ever: people came to see and buy boats.

Even with the success of the independent shows, it is the author's opinion that a review of the CNSS policies and attitudes might still produce a happier working agreement with exhibitors. However, time is running out, for there is already a smell in the air that the days of boat shows may be coming to an end.

The Sailing Game

Life in the Sailboat World

The Sailing Game

Life in the Sailboat World

Chapter 4

Sailing Champs

How a Champion is Made – The Hans Kreuz Story

One does not become a North American sailing champion from nothing. At 13, Hans was sailing in Düsseldorf, Germany, on the Rhine River:

My father had been a merchant ship officer, and my parents put me in a sailing club with a very active youth programme stressing the seamanship basics of handling and sailing.

I was also taught maintenance and repairs and, very importantly, the rules of the road on the frenetically busy Rhine [which is] crowded with large, long, and fast commercial traffic.

Each of us students was assigned a mentor, generally a yacht owner, and we crewed for our mentor for many years, absorbing the ins and outs of boating. I had to pass a written and practical test in order to obtain the mandatory Skipper's Licence for anyone in charge of a vessel on the Rhine.

My club owned some very popular European "Pirate" racing dinghies for the use of the youth students. We had to take care of these boats from every possible aspect and keep a detailed log. Two of the seniors taking me under their wing were many times European "Pirate" champions, and they taught me the finer tricks of the trade while racing in the club Pirates and other class boats such as the Star, BM-Jolle, Schaeren Cruiser, and Scharpie.

When I was 15, my father bought my brother and me an old Pirate, which we fixed up and raced under the handicaps of youth and poor boat condition. That year, I joined three other Pirates on a 14-day Star Cruise down the Rhine and into Holland, under orders to be back on the 14th day. Often we had to be towed, but

[we] kept up our daily log, which had to be signed by an official of a yacht club or the mayor, head of police, pharmacist, or doctor who lived in the area. Sometimes we kids slept at yacht clubs, but mainly in our Pirates. I still remember how the Dutch were so very helpful to us junior visitors.

After that character-forming trip I was off the water for six years. I worked as a lumber apprentice and did an 18-month stint in the German Army before emigrating to Canada. In 1966, I was overjoyed to be sailing again on Glenmore Reservoir in Calgary and made many friends fooling around in Fireballs and Flying Dutchmen and even started winning some races. I met Hubert Steghaus, a fellow German immigrant, who had a fully battened Flying Kitten, which he said he bought from Fred van Zuiden. He told me Fred was looking for crew. He and I started racing the FK against the Yachting Worlds, which had been the first cat class in Calgary. There were some real hot shots in that class, including Glen Mainland and his crew, Bert North, so we had some exhilarating competition along with fellow FK racers. I started working for Fred on a part time basis about 1967 and, the following year, joined the Glenmore Sailing Club, as well as starting full time at Glenmore Boats Ltd.

Fred and I started to race the FK seriously, both locally and out of town. I clearly remember the then famous Kelowna Blossom Time Regatta. We raced on handicap, as there were mostly not enough boats to form Classes. We did very well in those regattas and had a tremendous amount of fun. We all fell in love with the magnificent Okanagan Valley and its sweet smell of blossoms and gentle surrounding mountains: a fairy tale background for sailing and taking a break from work! It reminded us time and time again of the lush French Riviera, and the Blossom Regatta became implanted in our memories forever. Winemaking was in its infancy; coming to this hot lake saw us innocently overindulge many times and struggle to get up next day. We had the gratification of placing 1st and 2nd in our FK and still have many trophies and mugs to prove our youthful prowess, never mind overindulgence.

We spent a lot of time building up the FK's speed with improved battens and sleek underwater ship. In 1968 we felt we were ready for the World Multihull Championship and could well compete with the movers and shakers in the A, B, C, and D catamaran classes. Among those classes was a very fast single-hander by the name of Sea Spray, designed by Allan Arnold. Glenmore first imported a Sea Spray, then moved to assembling the parts, and took the final step of complete manufacturing. Conditions were different in Canada, and we immediately had to tackle changing the more efficient sock sail to the halyard system and needed to address other matters, which did not move smoothly over to the Canadian sailing scene.

Sea Spray sales took off, and the Class attracted a number of very good sailors. Names like Phil Ryan, an Australian who worked on his foils, Ed Michaud, an engineer always trying to lower the all-up weight, Barry Lester, another engineer who could just make her go, and Duuk van Heel, the most innovative skipper!

Picking up the loot at a Kelowna Blossom Time Regatta

Life in the Sailboat World

In later years, this lowering of boat weight was championed by another engineer, Dave West, for whom an argument could be made, destroyed the class by his fanatical weight reduction adherence.

The Americans had formed NASSA [North American Sea Spray Association] and put together some rough class rules. Ed Michaud and I tried to improve these rules for the CSSA [Canadian Sea Spray Association] in an attempt to maintain a strict one-design. At a later date, the Americans adopted the Canadian rules except for a few crucial differences, and it was not until about 40 years later that both agreed to uniform rules. The major bone of contention had been increasing the all-up weight to 180 lbs.

We managed to have our own class starts throughout Western Canada and held the 1st North American championship in 1971 in Calgary. We had an astonishing 38 cats at the starting line, and Larry Nord of San Francisco Bay was the first American in 5th place.

Duuk van Heel joined us in 1970 after the demise of a local competitor, and Glenmore added more boats to its stable with the Smallcraft 18, a copy of the English Osprey, the International Enterprise under license from the RYA [Royal Yachting Association], and the German designed Kolibri. We began handling cruisers such as the Aquarius and Ensenada out of California. We supplied fittings and sails and did repairs to all kinds of classes. Glenmore Boats was on the move!

While I became successful sailing the Sea Spray among fleets all over the Western Canadian and the USA, in fact the most challenging fleet was right in Calgary on Glenmore Reservoir, where fickle wind conditions dominated, from light to howling gales in minutes. One had to put harrowing concentration on wind shifts in order to take fast advantage. Most Glenmore sailors developed this ability and used it successfully time and time again on other bodies of water.

The Duuk Van Heel Racing Story

Duuk van Heel was a world, North American, Dutch, and Canadian national champion many times over. The following interview was taped August 1, 2002 at S'Graveland in the Netherlands.

In what years were you the world Flying Junior champion and where were these events raced?

The first time I became World Champion was in 1963 at San Remo, Italy, along with my crew, Kokkie van den Berg. In those days, the World Championships were sailed every 3 years...in 1965 at Sjortjur Baden near Stockholm along with crew, J.F van Ochtrop...the last time, during the 1967 Montreal World's Fair with crew, Marleen van Duin on Lac St Louis. Marleen's father was an Olympic Dragon Class sailor and approved the trip so she would get the opportunity to compete in what was then a long way from home.

Before we left for Montreal, I won the European championship in Garnac, France, again with van Ochtrop. In 1969, I got the World Championship for the 4th time sailing with Gerrie Kerstbergen at Pampas island near Muiden.

Pampus, actually a sand bank, was an interesting place in that its old fort protected Amsterdam in the Middle Ages. The merchant ships [that] came back from the Far East laden with seasoning, bamboo, and tobacco couldn't get into Amsterdam harbor because of that shallow water. A large barge was tied up on each side of the merchant ship and filled with water. The water was then pumped out of the barges and they floated the merchant ship high enough for it [to] go through the shallow water into the centre of Amsterdam harbour. It was a complicated maneuvre, but it worked.

I assume your parents encouraged you to start sailing; were they your only teachers or did you take independent sailing lessons?

In the days I was under ten, say six or seven, I went quite often

**Two fabulous champions
Hans Kreuz and Duuk van Heel**

with my father to Westeinder, a lake near Schiphol airport where the Dragon was very popular. They all left the marina to race, headed for an island-starting tower. I was often allowed to take the helm and was coached by both father and grandfather. Grandfather had a fairly large boat with wheel steering, which is more difficult than a tiller. On really large boats tiller steering becomes too heavy. You have to tune the helm 'till she is neutral like the old heavy and beamy fishing boats that had to balance their side-boards.

Did you naturally take to sailing or did your parents have to push you a little?

No, I wanted to sail, myself, always! When I was twelve I joined the Jantjes youth group of about 60 to 80 kids at the Royal Loosdrechtse Yacht Club. We got lessons in the names of fittings, rigging of all types of boats, anchoring, tying up to a buoy, man overboard procedure, reefing and so on.

Were your first racing efforts in Optimists?

No, the first racing was in the Dutch National Youth Boat "Fluff" (Pluis). Such a funny name for a two-person 12-foot boat. It was designed by van Essen, a bit like a small Flying Junior, but not very famous.

Do you feel that race training is more stringent today than in your youth?

It has become much more so. In those days we trained ourselves and, Sunday mornings, would rent a Fluff for $1.50 for the whole day. We sailed into the lake looking for other boats from the various yacht clubs and did unofficial races and tuning together. Saturday mornings we went to sailing class and in the afternoon trained with the Jantjes youth group. We were 8 to 10 years old, and the better sailors got a coach who taught the finer aspects of how to make a boat go faster and especially how to roll tack.

When was the Flying Dutchman (FD) designed?

The preliminary designs were out in 1951, and by 1957, it was selected after competition to replace the Sharpie at the 1960 Olympics. The 20-foot Tornado dinghy with wide decks and hard chine already existed as did the Sharpie and Valk designs. The Tornado was at the Royal Loosdrechtse Yacht Club and we Jantjes had access to them. It was truly a forerunner of the Flying Dutchman.

The Olympic Flying Dutchman was a fantastic, fast planing dinghy. It had among other things a genoa instead of a jib, which was larger than the mainsail. Almost 2,000 were built. The British made a movie, *Going for Gold*, which showed the FD planing at 25 miles per hour. I once paced FDs with my Sea Spray when the East Europeans were training on the Dutch Lakes and out sailed them around an Olympic course.

How strong is the Flying Junior class today and where is she concentrated?

The numbers have greatly decreased worldwide. I was there right at the start with boat number three, which had a measurement flaw, so the builder gave me a new boat. We started designing and making fittings and wind indicators at that time for our own boats and to earn income to buy a new hull. My next hull was already #303. There are a few thousand concentrated in Japan where they are used a great deal in training and sailing schools. The Japanese are good sailors; the Worlds were held there in 2001, and they took first and second places.

Are flying juniors still being built?

Perhaps there are one or two yards in Europe and one in Japan. The van Dusseldorf and van Wetten yards have not built them for the last few years, although the latter still builds his famous Optimist.

Which of your tactics made you a Flying Junior, Fireball, and Sea Spray champion?

I have been thinking quite a bit about this point. It is not just tactics; one of the important things is that you must sail your boat for many hours to get an intimate feel of how it best sails. This means you can always sail it at top speed and when you are able to do that, you have time to look around and make decisions about wind shifts and your best course. The most important thing, though, is to keep your boat at top speed. Trying to keep your boat at top speed during the start can be a bit messy and is often not possible with boats to windward and leeward. So you have to get out of the busy area, and the sooner the better. To get out you have to tack and tack again to be back on starboard. When you do this, you reach clear wind and can sail at top speed again while the others are still struggling with each other in dirty air with lots of "up, up" yelling and screaming on their lee and windward.

I seem to remember you very much liked centre of the line starts.

Very often, but in important races I often don't try to get the best starting position as a lot of sailors are on the same spot. It becomes crowded and it is questionable if you really are having a good start. A start can be ruined by someone who is over early and subsequently spoils your start. If that happens, it is hard to get out of the area. It is a real problem and is why I try to be out of the busy area, which is my favourite method to this day. I do not mind giving up 10 metres, which I generally make up in the next few minutes because of my free air. So, this is my preference and as I have good or better boat speed, I have double chance to end up on top.

At this stage in your life do you feel your racing tactics are even sharper?

No, because when you have a full time job and a busy family, your sailing time is measurably down. So, you lose a bit of your prowess. During my twenties, sailing the Flying Junior, I had sufficient sailing hours that I could feel immediately if I had picked up some weed, so would only lose a few metres. Now it takes time before I notice, as there is only a minuscule difference in boat speed in my 12-foot Jol. It is extremely sensitive to the smallest adjustment I make. Many things make me go a little slower than other boats and I do not feel it so instantly, but mainly it is the combination of not putting in the hours and not being in my twenties anymore.

I win the odd race following your sail low, sail fast techniques. When you are ahead nothing challenges you except a handicap rating! Are you still winning races?

Yes I am still winning some races, often in my 12-foot Jol.

Tell me about your racing in the Jol, and in the 30-foot wooden boat inherited from your grandfather.

The Jol was, I believe, designed in 1914 by the Englishman, George Cockshott, and was one of the first racing classes in the world.

Is the Jol class thinking of building it out of Coremat or similar material, or perhaps even rotary molding it to bring the price down and expand the class?

I don't decide these things, even though I am the Class secretary. There are about 340 members and about 240 boats in Europe. One of the goals of this very old class is to keep the boat as is and not to bring in any developments in the way of materials, fittings, foils, sizes of spars or anything. Once one starts allowing such things there is no end to it. The boats would become lighter because of a new material and then a bit later another lighter material or component would come into the Class, as I said, no end to it. Suddenly old boats are outdated. Not changing the boats results—like last week during our championship— [in] the two leading entries the first two days [having been] built in the twenties.

I agree there are pitfalls letting in new materials; I have seen it with Fireballs and my own Sea Spray class.

Life in the Sailboat World

We have had certain developments in the Jol Class such as building out of mahogany, oak, and cedar; one was built out of okumee. People have been trying to bring the weight of the boat down, but that was stopped about six years ago. The hull weight is being maintained at 104kg, and you may say that is quite heavy. It includes the few fittings, but not the foils, spars, or sails. Lighter boats have to take on lead weights. The idea is to keep the old boats competing. We have an Italian fibreglass, lighter version with wooden seats, stainless steel centreboard, and different rudder system. They can't compete with us in Holland, because of the lighter weight. We can compete in Italy, but what is the use, we were losing all the time.

I think you are doing the right thing when I see the downfall of some classes.

Because of new developments in sails back and forth between Dacron and Mylar, people had to keep buying new sails. The funny thing is that I had my boat built in 1989 and sailed it with a home made sail. Then in 1993 I bought a professionally made sail and still use it. Some owners keep buying new sails every two or three years, but as long as I can be competitive with my present sail, why buy a new one.

Are you winning 80% of the races in which you participate?

That is difficult to say, but I think at least half. In the other races, I am usually in the top three but sometimes end up fourth. In the 2002 Nationals, in seven races I ended up in third out of 41 boats because I could only drop one of a 15th and two 16th places. There is very competitive racing created by good old boats performing as well as the new boats.

Are you able to attract young sailors at a time when many classes are suffering from lack of new blood?

Our top sailor is about 28 years and the second around 23, and compared to my age, they are young. We do not attract many young sailors and there is no large influx. What we do see is sailors leaving other Classes where they have been successful, like Laser or the Dutch Valk, Pampus, BM16, Vrijheid etc., and joining

Jol. At a certain moment, they seem to say to hell with their Class and yearn to get back to the basics.

The Jol is truly back to one-design basics with its one sail, but even so, every boat is a little different because it is hand-made in the true sense of the word. There can be disparities in the hull radius because no piece of wood is the same as the next. Some planks are wider than others, and as well you can never get the chines the same. We find differences in width and overall length up to a couple of centimetres. The Jol is not built in a mold, but crafted around a hull shape; it is quite amazing to see how it is done, but they have become very expensive to build.

In 2000 I think you said the boats were about $17,500 Cdn.

They are a lot higher now, more like $22,000 Cdn, and when one goes into exotic wood, the price can be $25,000. Mahogany is used, or the very expensive cedar, but the latter is very soft and dents easily, so don't hit anything!

What are the dominant one-design racing classes in Europe? We saw the Iso and the Buzz racing in England; they looked like miniature 49ers.

I can tell you in Holland it is the Optimist for youth sailing. When they grow out of that, they go to the Splash and then Laser. Girls go into the Europe and men often to the Finn from the Laser. The Finn is very popular in Loosdrecht, but the Splash is increasingly popular for youth sailing. It's built in Northern Holland by Roel Wester and there are already over 2,000 with well organized competition. Another popular class is the Pampus, at least in Loosdrecht, a two man 23-footer wooden keel with 2.6-foot draft.

You said that a lot of Classes in the last thirty years have declined or virtually disappeared.

Many of the old classes such as the BM or the Sixteen Square Metre are still there, but don't have the activity of the newer classes. A few times each year they get together and have Regattas. In my early twenties, when I was at university, there were big sailing weeks all over Holland. To name a few: the Westeinder, the Weeks at Brasumer, the Kaag, the Nieuw Loosdrecht, the Holland, the

Muiden 2nd Week, the Alkmaarder, and last, but not least, the Sneak Week [also of ice skating fame]. In those regattas, 300 to 800 sailboats would participate, and now you are likely to see between 50 and 450 boats. The one exception is Sneak Week, which for some unknown reason still pulls in about a thousand boats. The Zieriksee is also well attended, but it is mainly for the social side of things.

What has come in place of these event weeks are the big International Meets like the SPA Regatta in Medemblik, Holland; Kiel Week in Germany; Poole, UK; Hyere, France; Smyrna, Turkey; Kingston in Canada, and some others just for Olympic and national classes. They attract international sailors from Canada, USA, Japan, Australia, and all European countries. These regattas have become a "must do" circuit in order to train and win your birth in the Olympic games. These regattas are typically in the same form we had for national level class racing, but there are not so many because only Olympic classes are participating.

Have you seen the Iso and Buzz in Holland?

No. We have about 10 to12 49ers and a few 29ers, but Hollanders have not taken to these non-Dutch style designs; interest is low even at the Medemblik Olympic training event, where you might only find competition for about 30 to 40 boats.

One-design racing has diminished in Canada and it is a struggle to get good numbers at championships, and regular regattas. Is it the same in Holland?

Yes, it seems to be that way here, too, and it looks also like professionalism is creeping into the sailing sport. And because of that, the professionals sail in most major events and sail all year around. They are being sponsored with the idea that, if they keep sailing, they can climb up to the Olympics after participating at Spa, Hyere, Poole, Kiel, etc. That means that people who want to sail as a sport on the weekend, the engineers, lawyers, doctors, truck drivers, pilots, bankers, clerks, etc. have become amateur sailors in their own class. The sailing world has split into two arms, the amateurs and professionals.

Life in the Sailboat World

Are you accusing the sailors in the Olympic sail-offs of being professionals, trying to acquire fame and all that goes with it?

Yes I am. I mean, once someone becomes an Olympic champion, they are courted by sport clothing manufacturers and sail makers to endorse their products. They are making use of you or commercializing you. When their sailing days are over, they open up a clothing or sport shop and use their name to advantage.

I wonder if I was abusing the system in my racing days.

No, you were never that good of a sailor. You were good in selling and promoting your product and management. In the early sixties, sailing was not that sophisticated. Now, they are even allowing advertising on boats, and that will open up another can of worms.

What also has become a major problem is people having less spare time and being overburdened with all kinds of other things. When I think of my family, there are other sports like golf to do on a weekend, or my wife wants to go to the coast or make a quick trip to visit museums in Rome or Paris. It all takes organization and time away from sailing. You might say the sport has become a victim of good times, and high living is claiming sailors.

On that note the interesting interview came to an end. Duuk, a fine sailor, always willing to pass on his secrets, has a great sense of humour, duty, and generosity.

The Sailing Game

Life in the Sailboat World

Chapter 5

Our Sales Swell

Dealing With Dealers

In the seventies, we sold through a dealer network, and one of our favourites was Rob Griffel of Pigeon Lake, who regularly ordered 20 to 30 Sea Sprays a year. Rob was a colourful character born in Hamburg, who built his very own "Flying Dutchman," a device on four wheels propelled by pumping one's arms and steering with one's legs. He took it all through Holland in the twenties while on holidays from his boatbuilding job.

In the thirties, he contracted to build dinghies for the king of Romania and at the same time train their youth for the Olympics. All came to an end in 1941 when Germany invaded the Soviet Union; our hero was drafted deep into Russia to help the engineering corps build bridges along the fluid Caucasus front lines. After the Stalingrad debacle, the Germans retreated to the Kuban Peninsula with heavy Tiger and Panther [trade name, not German panzer] tanks and found their backs to the sea. Rob came to the rescue and was commissioned to construct giant rafts out of oil barrels; men, tanks, and guns rolled onto the rafts and escaped over the Straight of Azov.

His luck ran out in Western Russia and he spent five years as a prisoner of war in a Baltic country. Not one to waste time, he taught wood carving to fellow prisoners and villagers and earned brownie points towards an earlier release. Back in Germany, he advertised for his lost wife, and together they emigrated to Canada.

His memory and talent still surround me in the form of carved sailors and beautiful trophies for the Sea Spray Class, along with my oil portrait by his talented daughter.

In the early days, we took Rob's lake front lots for payment, which we quickly sold for at least $1,000 each to finance more boat building, lots which now go for over half a million. We had some fine regattas on Pigeon Lake, and at one event, Mr. Justice Manning served magnificent one-inch barbequed steaks. My brother Wim, visiting from Holland, talks to this day about those steaks as the highlight of the regatta (mine too!).

Despite his success, the years were passing, and Rob sold out to a trio of Edmonton 25-year-olds, each with a university degree. For a while, they kept Rob's lake premises and opened a tent outlet in west Edmonton. We were fascinated by their MBA ideas, but worried about double overhead, winter season closing, and three bosses. Our experience taught us business is done throughout the winter with fittings, repairs, and gifts, as well as people visiting the boat showroom to see how to spend bonuses, tax rebates, and holiday money. We offered winter deals and took many deposits throughout the slow season.

The new guys expanded and took on larger cruisers, for which there was a market on larger lakes near Edmonton. They continued to give Glenmore substantial orders, but in the summer of 1980 when I delivered half their annual order, I was told to cancel the balance. I protested vigorously, as we had built the whole order, with the balance sitting ready for delivery. I felt hit by a bomb and let John know I felt his actions unethical and that he was not well advised to lose the confidence of his suppliers. I surmised he had over-

Rob Griffel, the dealer who built boats for the king of Romania

purchased in eastern Canada, but he claimed sales were falling. I did not realize it immediately, but this was our first glimpse of the decline in the economy, which, in turn, was to lead to receivership.

There was inevitable strife between partners, and one by one they left, and the company disintegrated. It was a sad situation that a major city like Edmonton was not serviced by a sailboat outlet, and with minor short-lived backyard exceptions, no full time dealership appeared for twenty years. It takes mighty effort, dedication, time, capital, and street smarts to survive in a space-intensive business, which, if you are lucky, has a 5-month sales season. It was also my first glimpse of a changing business environment where the motivator was what variant of grey can I get away with. Glenmore picked up the void and serviced Edmonton sailors.

I came across another stunt in the bustling city of Kelowna, where a new dealer had ordered 12 catamarans. I delivered the rig to their yard after driving 650 km (400 miles), and they closed the gate behind me. I wondered what was next, and when I stepped into the owner's office, I was told they would take only 8 of the 12 boats ordered. Once again, I protested with vigour, but the best I could do was cancel their free freight, and we didn't deal with them again. They too disappeared from the marine scene in a short while.

I decided to salve my soul by going home via the #3 highway, a spectacular, quiet road winding through incredible scenery from mountain to desert, dark browns to lush greens, and overpowering slates and blacks. The deep canyons with rivers far below terrorized me as I tried to hang on to hairpin curves, all a test for man and machinery screaming to be conquered.

I stopped at Cranbrook for a recovery lunch and found someone studying the four lonesome catamarans. He said he had a market for them and bought them then and there at my best dealer price, and so I arrived home with an empty trailer. Ah, the mysteries of life!

California Ventures 1980

A Calgary investors' group, including Marius van Ellenburg and Henk van Buren, approached Glenmore to operate a US company to make Sea Sprays and the 11 ft. Sesame dinghy. The group had the opportunity to buy the US rights and molds and wanted to repeat the Canadian success. We invested, as well as committing to provide building supervision and management. A plant was rented in Santa Ana and a manager appointed, but immediately we found operating in the US was totally different. The banks were not at all cooperative, despite our well funded venture and were suspicious of the fact we were Canadians. We found absentee management was not working and, even though Calgary to Los Angeles was a two-hour flight, it was not enough to effectively control the manufacturing process. Quality control was our prime goal, and we were not getting it from our manager who had trouble supervising the Mexican fibregass workers, good as they were. Inferior product reared its ugly head.

In the meantime, the American Group sent me to the huge Dusseldorf Boat Show, then the largest in the world, with 14 salons, where I had previously exhibited. This time I sold a container of Sea Sprays to Mannheim, West Germany, but the story did not end successfully. The German buyer opened the shipment and claimed it was impossible to assemble the ill-fitting pieces into sailboats.

We sent our good friend Duuk van Heel from Holland to straighten out the mess. He invoiced a reasonable fee, but added we had a problem on our hands in Southern California, and he was right.

While at the 1981 Toronto show, we came across a Sesame from our Santa Ana plant under the new name of Arrow. It appeared a Toronto dentist had paid our American manager $5,000 for the molds and, in partnership with our old friend Marv, was building our boat in Canada. Needless to say, the money did not find our Santa Ana bank account. We also learned the dentist had been offered the Freestyle 474 as an improved version of the Sea Spray. Our "manager" had secretly developed Freestyle at our Santa Ana plant.

After the first year's statements showed a five figure loss, we sold out, and Glenmore California was sold to a party south of San Francisco. Our manager ended up marrying Robbie Harvie's sister, and then we lost sight of him. Robbie Harvie was a famous Sea Spray sailor, who, in the USA One-of-a-Kind in horrendous winds, beat all other small cats, such as the Hobie 14, Solcat 15, and the Dart Uni Rig.

Robbie always claimed the Sea Spray and the Aquarius C Class were the only properly balanced cats he ever sailed. The Aquarius, with Alex Kozloff and Robbie on board, raced to victory against the Aussies, taking the Little America Cup, the premier trophy in the C Class world. The UK, USA, and Australia continually fought for it and, in 1996, Steve Clark returned it to the Americans. I am watching for the next challenger and note a greater depth of multihull development in Europe and Scandinavia and even Russia.

The Osprey Affair –
an Expensive English Experience

My partner, Audrey, English by birth, always claimed you had to watch your back when doing business with the English. Well, let me tell you about the Osprey molds affair. By 1980, we felt the need for a high performance 18 ft. dinghy in our line up and decided the English Osprey was the answer. The boat was already somewhat known here, as Smallcraft had been making an unauthorized copy named the SC18. The Osprey had the reputation of out sailing the Olympic Flying Dutchman, especially in the heavy weather and strong tides around the Isle of Wight.

We wrote to Ian Proctor, the designer. We had previously bought his masts and had a mutual friend in his neighbour, Brian Crawley, our old production manager and dealer. Ian thought we might be interested in a virtually new set of molds sitting at Westerley Boat Works, from which had come two successful hulls. He quoted $5,000 for the molds and a completed black hull to help spread freight costs and to use as a guide. Proctor's other famous dinghies were the Wayfarer, now built by Abbott in Sarnia, the Hornet, Flying 15, and the Olympic Tempest.

We went to the UK as Ian's guest while inspecting the molds and were repeatedly told there were no problems. That should have put us on our guard.

Everything arrived at our Airdrie plant and our production manager, Jim, who had an extensive background in the fibreglass industry, went to work on the Osprey. In fact, he worked on it exclusively for at least three months, and nothing else came off the production line. I was perturbed and, like a clap thunder, Jim told me the deck mold did not fit the hull; it was impossible to make an acceptable Osprey.

We wrote Proctor, explaining the unpleasant discovery and demanded a refund. To this day, we are still waiting for an answer and the funds. I sometimes wondered if this had something to do with Smallcraft copying his Osprey, for which he never got royalties; after all, we were both Calgary companies. Ian Proctor died recently; I hope he is sailing in fair winds.

We offered the Osprey molds at no cost to interested sailing clubs and, lo and behold, an English group from the west coast wanted to acquire them, but nothing materialized. It is something like ashes to English ashes.

Dealing With Dealers II – The Roof Caves In

In 1982, President Reagan oversaw interest at US banks going to 20%, which meant 25% in Canada. My phone rang off the wall; virtually all my dealers said the same thing, "with interest at this level, we cannot sell boats; cancel the order and keep the deposit." I had 200 pre-ordered boats in production, and the raw components were on order, sitting on our shelves or already in a finished boat.

Life in the Sailboat World

It was time to talk to our friendly bank manager, Tim McMoneybags, who had impressed on us if we ever hit a rough spot to talk it over with him. We drove three nervous blocks across the Bow River to explain our predicament; we had not yet taken up our full credit line and had 4:1 asset coverage of the loan. We suggested a temporary loan extension as funds would come in slower in a soft consumer market. He promised to get back.

He had already stopped payment on a $2.34 cheque as we drove back to our office, and we smelled trouble with a capital T. He called a few hours later said we should be at the bank at 9:00 the following morning. At this meeting, we found Coopers & Lybrand, trustees in bankruptcy, and their solicitor; we had taken along our auditor. The meeting got off to a touchy start when Audrey, full of suggestions, was told by the solicitor to keep quiet and await the outcome of the meeting. It was decided to place Glenmore Boats in receivership and to appoint Coopers & Lybrand the receiver for the Toronto Dominion Bank. I was to fire the entire plant staff and shut down the Airdrie plant, and was told that a locksmith would be there at 8.00 a.m. to change the locks.

I was asked if I wanted security protection while firing the staff, but I declined. I told the staff of the bank's decision and said they should pick up pay cheques the following day. I wished the production manager good luck and was told he did not need my good luck! He was piqued because he and his family had taken salaries through their company to save taxes and therefore, were just another creditor, not open to the protection of employee wages.

The same morning, Cooper's senior man George Kozlowski, CA, moved into our office and was charged with raising the money to repay the bank. We had various meetings with George and the insolvency CA's at Cooper & Lybrand and were asked to present a plan to raise funds for the bank.

We retired for the weekend to a hideaway in the Columbia River Valley. We sat on the lawn in front of our unit with majestic

Nobody buys boats at summer's end- not even at $999!

mountains as a back drop and put our smartest thoughts on paper to save our company from oblivion. We drew up a plan to sell inventory and finish incomplete boats, which would produce sufficient to repay the bank and then some! Remember, we had a very high ratio of asset to debt. George, our "keeper" from Coopers, had a very clear mind and was a good listener. Audrey and he hit it off right away, probably because they were both dedicated bean counters. George easily saw that no funds had been frittered away and that our plan was feasible. I had poetically told George our ship would not go under, but he would only say, with a bit of a smile on his face, we would have to see about that.

In response to advertised invitations to buy our assets, there were a few loony responses, and an auctioneer offered 5% recovery. We and our auditor, Don Flood, had a very serious meeting at the Cooper offices. They quickly recognized our assets would remain valueless without our nurturing hand to sell them. It was like a death reprieve when Coopers' chief, Barry Hunt, said they would go along with our proposal for the time being. We wanted to celebrate, but it seemed indecent at that point.

The bank, through Coopers, would finance the continued operation of our retail premises in downtown Calgary. We would sell direct to the public at an initial discount of 20% and were to drop our dealer network, which had contributed to our downfall. We were authorized to increase boat discounts to 35%, if needed, and give up to 40% off fittings, spars, and accessories.

The public liked the attractive prices, and we were inundated with customers who ran us off our feet—the money poured in. If I were to analyze our success, in hindsight, it was that we were forced into receivership before all the mortgage foreclosures started. People who later became jaded with the numerous receivership sales still felt they were getting excellent deals from Glenmore, and they really were!

After two weeks of close collaboration, George K pulled out and gave us the keys. He thought we had a well-run organization, were honest, and could be left to do our own thing. He asked us to call him if we needed to spend over $5,000. Coopers topped up our battery company bank account, which allowed us to pay day-to-day expenses. If we needed payroll or larger cheques signed, they did so without hesitation. It worried us that we could not settle our old accounts payable, but were told in no uncertain terms we stood liable to prosecution if we did so.

We suffered a vicious assault from another direction. Alberta Opportunity Company (AOC), who held the second mortgage on the Airdrie plant, called from the Ponoka Head Office and suggested we had better pay up or they would seize all assets, including wedding bands and bikes! They ultimately sold our plant and, along with Royal Trust, got their mortgage money.

We evacuated the plant and put our 18-year-old summer student, William Austin, in charge. He did a fantastic job for one so young, moving heavy molds, spraying equipment, about 250 finished boats, parts, and lots of aluminum to our downtown premises. He did it in one week with a minimum of damage and help. He was splendid!

We kept operating and selling. Many of the hurt creditors were happy to do business again, once they were comfortable Coopers would sign the cheques or if we paid them hard cash. The only exception was a major Canadian fibreglass supplier who never relented, so we just went somewhere else! Generally, the marine industry understood what happened.

A close associate, Dieter Schlaffke, and his wife helped finish the boats or built new product. We had just got a contract to build motorized miniature airplanes for the Alhazar Stampede parade, but without men and plant it was impossible. Dieter took over the contract. I had always wanted to spread our product base, but now it was too late. A high TD Bank executive, seeing we were well on the way to repaying the loan, speculated his bank had been hasty in ordering the receivership and had reacted too fast to an inexperienced manager who had panicked. This same now-retired executive honed his sailing skills on one of our boats; he became so good, he sailed the Atlantic single-handed in his 27 ft. (8.23 m) C&C. He was also the first to order a copy of my book and gave me hope and courage to keep writing.

It may sound odd, but we were never mad at the bank or at the receiver. It was their money, and we undertook to repay it. In the early eighties, a deal was still a deal, and the term renegotiate was not bandied around; they had to protect their threatened position.

Frankly, after the initial shock, we found the receivership period an exhilarating business management learning experience. We will forever be indebted to Cooper's George Kozlowski for teaching us so much and supporting our efforts. After 15 months of hard bargaining with the public, we paid the bank principal funds of $450,000, but no interest, and were discharged from receivership. The receiver got some $50,000 for its trouble and was so pleased with our performance, they recommended us to the Royal Bank, with whom we worked for the next twenty profitable years.

Supplying the Department of National Defence

In the mid-nineties we got many DND contracts for large numbers of our Kolibri 2-12 trainer and these contracts brought another level of maturity to our operations. For the first time, we had to meet ISO 9002 specifications, operate under NATO requirements, and make sure all hulls came off the line within one pound of each other, as in Olympic standards. We were forced to give demonstrations to prove the Kolibri, even when swamped, would still float above the water line. The Calgary Yacht Club was generous enough to let us use their facilities, and I can tell you we went through a few nervous moments with the inspector watching our every move. The requirements left little tolerances, but we passed the test.

It was a good thing we had two sets of molds. Each mold could be cycled three times per six-day week, so we could count on about 25 boats per month. Initially, we subcontracted the fibreglass work to a Lethbridge plant, who soon found the higher standards needed for sailboat work were radically increasing their costs. Our DND contracts did not allow for price changes, so we searched and found a first rate firm in Red Deer who understood that higher standards had to be met. Even so, they went through a curve adjusting their thinking from RV bodies, slides, holding tanks, and hot tubs. We had a few problems with weight tolerances and precision, but they ended up meeting those standards beautifully.

We often had five or six hulls spread over the shop floor, being simultaneously fitted out by our long term employee, Martin. Another long-time associate, Gary, did the quality control and the piles of DND paperwork. Over a span of five years, we shipped hundreds of Kolibri 2-12s, which we were under the gun to deliver by the March 31 federal fiscal year end.

This mid-winter delivery date caused us lots of problems. We often worked in -22°F (–30° C) temperatures, loading boats on racks in 53 ft. (16.15 m) containers and had to use heaters to pre-vent workers from freezing. We shipped with both CPR and CNR and learned a whole new art of loading properly and dealing with inspectors who snapped photos all over the place, building defences against damage law suits. Year after year, containers left for bases in Ontario, Nova Scotia, Newfoundland, and Quebec, but sometimes luck runs out. It was not a nice morning when the Trois Rivières base phoned to tell us they had opened a container and found the racking splintered and the boats mangled. They refused acceptance and told us the rail agent was already denying rough handling and shunting. Of course, of course!

We had utilized this manner of loading for years without damage, but the best the rail company would promise was to return the container and reship at no charge.

We carefully unloaded the container and found the situation, with all the drama removed, to be not that bad. Of the twelve Kolibris, six were actually unscratched. Four had damage that the Red Deer company repaired perfectly, and two boats need to be replaced. Twelve boats went back to Trois Rivières stronger than ever, and our insurance paid the repair costs. The severely dam-aged boats were repaired and sold at a good discount; the buyers found the DND grey to be good camouflage when they went hunt-ing!

The foregoing drama was all over in thirty days, and once again, what seemed a gut wrenching tragedy was dealt with with-out losing our heads. We were all stronger for the experience. One decision we made as a result was that if we could make our own deliveries in the west, we would. We found Jeeps were good workhorses, and we built a variety of racks and trailers to take dif-ferent boat combinations. The secret was good tie-downs and con-tinual checking throughout the trip.

Our ad hoc trucking company led us through some bizarre experiences. Once, a trucker pulled me over and told me a boat had bounced off my trailer and hit the ditch. I did a quick U- turn and found it 6 miles (10 km) back, luckily in a snow filled ditch, which cushioned the fall. A fellow stood there studying what he thought was a windfall, but he helped me get it back on the trailer—albeit reluctantly. I doubt if there was $10 damage: another testament to the strength of our boats.

We did one delivery to a base in Fort Qu'Appelle. The radio reminded us a cold front was moving in, but we left Medicine Hat with good spirits, a full tank, and hot soup. Then it started snowing, blinding us in horrendous drifts and gusts. We slowed to less than 30 mph. (50 km/h) and passed many vehicles in the ditch. Screaming ambulances passed us in eerie snowstorm light, and I crossed my fingers as I watched my heavily strained wipers. I stopped and fought to open the door and, with axe and shovel, removed the snow build-up on boats and wheels. I thought I would pass out in the –22° F (–30° C) temperature and 37 mph. (60 km/h) winds; they inflicted a murderously chilling cold.

There was no shelter, so we kept moving and made Regina, reeling under 12 in. (30 cm) of snow. Old dealer friends, Phil and Maxyne Dawson, opened their warm house and brought us back to life. The highway was now closed!

We made Fort Qu'Appelle next day, still suffering –22° F (–30° C) temps, having warned the commander we needed four men to unload. However, the men would not come out in these conditions, and you can't blame them, especially as it was now –31° F (–35° C) in the valley. The commander and I did the unloading, walking down one boat at a time after fighting to cut the tie downs caked with salt and ice. You can do anything if you try, but we froze ourselves silly doing it. A minimum of words were spoken to save body heat, and I thought the Lord was taking revenge for us working on Sunday, when we could have been in church listening to a sermon.

After hot fish soup at the canteen, we were thankful to head home via the reopened highway. We couldn't believe our bad luck when the weather deteriorated west of Regina; we could no longer see the lanes, the ditches belligerently inviting us in. Semis and busses still felt it expedient to pass and gave us heart-stopping

Life in the Sailboat World

moments of blindness and near-to-death breathlessness. At times, Audrey instructed me through her open window "left...left...no to the right... more to far left...a bit right...more right. How much longer could we go through this? We were by now both totally drained zombies. Pulling off the highway was not an option: the headlights behind us would soon crush us.

The tide turned at Maple Creek; we tanked up and took off with 40 units behind, including a little old lady who had apparently been behind us earlier. It was not the first time I broke trail, but this was hair-raising, and I wondered why this southwest corner of Saskatchewan was so riddled with terrible blizzards and bone-chilling, howling winds. Snow at least gives traction, but nothing saves you from beautifully polished black ice.

An Arizona friend asked if I really needed more of these winter adventures, but somehow we survive them and go on to enjoy the other good things Canada offers.

Another Look at Receivership

A receivership in the eighties was not the frightening catastrophe you might originally think. If you have marketable assets and good management, you can mount a rescue. Suppliers will do business with you again, perhaps COD initially, because they are anxious to start recouping their losses.

We were continually fed good financial advice from our chartered accountant, Don Flood, a rock we really leaned on. Our losses were quietly used to tax advantage, as Don dug out all the loopholes. Even the province helped, when it allowed us to qualify for the high interest rebate once we were out of receivership. We learned never again to tolerate demanding production workers and bullying managers. We were conditioned never to order goods that couldn't be paid for on the spot.

We lost our precious Airdrie plant, our so called retirement plan, but as they say you win some and lose some and perhaps learn from your mistakes. We henceforth contracted out fibreglass work to reputable plants and achieved absolute control on costs and could reject substandard products. We trained a few key workers to ISO standards and significantly reduced our payroll. Even currently, Glenmore still has components worth a small fortune ordered by plant staff in 1980. You don't worry so much about spending when it is not your money. I know there are unscrupulous operators who abuse receiverships, but all I can say is Glenmore Boats was not in that category.

The Escape Backstabbing

A new kid was on the block: the rotary molded sailboat. The Escape Boat company, with much fanfare, produced the 11 ft. (3.35 m) Captiva in 1993. The first one arrived in battleship grey, and we wondered how it would be seen upside down in the water. At least insects didn't like it and dirty marks were disguised! The Captiva had many innovative features, including a one-hour self teach system. This was stretching it a bit, maybe an afternoon, but I felt they were on the right track. It is a big hindrance to boat sales that a customer has to make a decision to go out and learn to sail, although some think they can learn on the web and be a champion the next day. The Captiva caught the public's imagination, and thousands were sold and introduced people to sailing. In fact, the Captiva became the best selling sailboat in its second year, and her sister, the Rumba, was named Boat of the Year in 1999.

A novice frightened by the wind can easily decrease the sail area by furling it around the mast. The bow shape of the Captiva cut through the water like old Corvettes, driving it under the hull so that the tendency to capsize was counteracted. Its crowning glory, however, were the two control lines instead of the mass of ropes that mystify new sailors.

Peter Johnston, CEO of Escape Boats, (our Henry Ford of the water) promoted the masses into sailing. His molded polyethylene boats were a third cheaper and a lot tougher. Like with any new thinking, there was a learning curve that resulted in embarrassing problems, but Escape stood behind their products and more than looked after us. Cindy led their top notch customer service area to overcome initial headaches, and we continued to make huge sales of seven different models.

In the fall of 1997, Escape offered a terrific price deal along with additional warranties and easy terms, enabling us to buy our 1998 supply at an unprecedented cost base. We should have smelled a fly in the ointment.

Later in '97 we were contacted by Huston-Barrett Leisure Products, a huge Canadian distributor, for whom we had high respect. They had never touched sailboats. Huston had become the Escape Canadian distributor, and suddenly Escape prices leaped hundreds of dollars, losing their price advantage. Huston had anticipated we would be a major customer, but were shocked when advised we had just bought all our 1998 boats (probably while they were negotiating the Canadian rights with Escape).

It puzzled us that a distributor totally ignorant of the industry could be persuaded to take on sailboats, but I suppose they considered them just another marine product. Nobody made it clear that sailboats are a totally different field of knowledge. Huston's people attended a "hoopla-hoopla" in Florida and went out on a sailboat for the first time. Glenmore's staff later helped them at shows to rig and "talk" sailboats.

After a few years, the Escape company was in trouble. I had seen the same trouble at four other rotary manufacturers; the methodology churns out a high volume of product, for which there is not a big enough market. Escape was taken over by the huge Johnson Outdoors conglomerate, and Peter Johnston was shipped to Wisconsin to aid the process.

By 2001, our Escape sales were slipping, even though they had brought out the innovative Playcat, SAIL Magazine's Catamaran of the Year. I understand the Escape product is still alive, but it is not easy to find parts.

Life in the Sailboat World

Manufacturer's Questionable Steps

It is hard to believe we sold Pelican pedal boats for some twenty years, but the market got bigger every time a new subdivision was built around a lake. Often, relations were stressed when Pelican set up other dealers in Calgary or made direct sales to institutions. Dealers launched a minor rebellion when they sold below our cost to big box retailers like Costco; ultimately they wiped out their huge dealer network. They were full of tricks designed to bypass legitimate dealers. They renamed products for firms like Canadian Tire, to sell as house brands or denied us the right to buy their lower priced paddleboats. I had bad dreams about consumers buying factory direct via the web, requiring minimal shipping staff and low overhead. We kept doing business with these rascals because somehow we still kept a small share of the pie.

In the fall of 1996, we received the *coup de grâce* letter from Noel Basque, Pelican's sales manager. We could no longer buy factory direct and were to purchase through Hunter Marine & RV, a huge Edmonton distributor, previously a Pelican dealer like ourselves. Pelican claimed sales would be more efficient through central stock points. We thought they had all the business they could handle, selling Costco more than 5,000 units a year. Dealers began dropping away because none could compete with Costco. We pleaded with Pelican to maintain our twenty-year relationship and were unsettled at being forced to deal with Hunter, a former competitor, who had also just opened a branch in Calgary.

Things have a habit of turning out for the best. It seems Hunter had also had its share of Pelican aggravations and saw Glenmore as an ally. They ended up selling us pedal boats at their cost, because by combining our needs, they were able to increase their annual order and buy at even better prices. We developed a very strong relationship with Hunter, and both of us made hay servicing all the Costco boats.

Life in the Sailboat World

Just the same, we were being squeezed, and our annual unit sales were slipping. It was time to look for other water toys, and off we went to the '97 Toronto Boat Show.

It was like the Lord knew we were coming. The Future Beach Company of Montreal was exhibiting new products like nothing anybody had seen before. Their super sales manager, Steve Oles, enthusiastically introduced us to two- and four-seater pedal boats and leisure kayaks. They were bright yellow and looked like they had arrived from outer space. They reminded us of the new futuristic VW, and, in fact, until Volkswagen got into the act, the new paddleboats were called Waterbeetles.

We had an instant love affair with Steve Oles, formerly Zodiac's Sales Manager — professional salespeople somehow sense each other. I suppose when Steve saw me climbing under and over the products, we both knew the standard ploy of disinterest was a

Future Beach's innovative Water Bee Paddle Boat

waste of time. When my eyes first feasted on these futuristic toys, I told Audrey I thought we had found a sweet replacement for Pelican and she agreed. More about the Future Beach company later, but suffice it to say we sold three 53 ft. container loads in the first year alone and ultimately became their largest dealer year after year. The icing on the cake was that Pelican was back within two years, begging us to buy directly from them again.

It was a province-wide shock when Hunter Marine went bankrupt to the tune of fourteen million dollars. It was even more of a shock to Pelican, who were also getting rattled at the news filtering back east that we were selling hundreds of Future Beach pedal boats all over Western Canada. Pelican management had relied on their market stronghold and had not noticed that competitors were producing vastly different products. The public could easily see the major improvements, and it was not difficult to sell these new-age pedal boats even at higher pricing. Rental outfits adored Water Bees, which were self-draining and didn't need to be emptied each morning. They carried more people and were absurdly stable, even on ocean waves.

Originally, we did not want their Waterskate kayak, designed by the Ontario Life Saving Society. It was a kayak which was extremely hard to capsize and gave children a greater sense of security at young people's camps. It was sit on-top, dry, and had twin catamaran hulls, which were the secret of its stability. Steve Oles insisted his products be under one roof, and suddenly we were in the kayak business, starting gingerly with three boats.

Once word got out they really were stable and very inexpensive, they became an instant success, and we sold hundreds. Nervous people, including Grandma, found themselves happy to get out on water. We saw the phenomenon that families would fight over the one kayak and came back for several more; after all, they were cheap enough. They were light, tracked well, but were not meant for white water.

We, who had never kayaked, took two down a benign stretch of the Columbia River to Radium Hot Springs, British Columbia.

The route through uninhabited wetlands full of eagles, ospreys, and bears was quite surreal. Audrey claims one mama bear had red eyes. There were no landing places en route, but towards the end of the 22-mile run (35.40 km), it got very windy, with sheets of rain and huge waves. We hid the kayaks overnight, climbed a goat path to civilization, and caught a taxi home! We rescued the kayaks next day, but not without jumping in the water to save the boats from the current. At a late stage in life, we had fallen in love with leisure kayaking.

Too Many Close Calls for Comfort

Anybody making their living on the road has close calls. I think my worst was near Winnipeg, when blinding snow was cutting vision and I was already passing vehicles in the ditch. A big gust blew all the loose snow in the world at me, and before I knew it, I was precariously in the ditch, too, at a 15-degree angle. My immediate worry was that another vehicle would land on me, and I did my best, with low gears, to climb out. Now, I know what being compacted in an avalanche means. I got the door open enough to squeeze out with my bag and suddenly heard a voice from above offering me a farmhouse bed for the night. I gratefully accepted yet another example of prairie hospitality. My hosts warmed me up with coffee and sandwiches, gave me a lovely bed and a great breakfast, to boot! The farmer organized a tow, and as I climbed back to the wheel, I saw my wallet in the snow, full of cash from boats sold at the show and lying there peacefully all night. My charmed life at work again!

I remember the sickening feeling of being airborne in Regina. The boat show people needed the hall and without mercy insisted I tie down outside, where the usual prairie snowstorm was raging. It was freezing, and the wind bit my face as I climbed at least 10 ft. (3 m) to reach the top trailer layer. Suddenly, I lost my footing and crashed down onto the ice strewn concrete parking lot. Not a soul saw me. I could either cry or try to get up, and that's what I did. No concussion, no bones broken, and I made it back, whistling all the way to Calgary.

Vanderstadt & McGruer was a long standing, highly regarded sailboat manufacturer who, in their time, must have put out thousands of sailboats, from small dinghies to 26-footers (7.92 m). They were a major force in Owen Sound and expanded their operations to a huge marina, restaurants, and service facilities. We dealt in their 17 ft. (5.18 m) Siren overnighter, which arrived seven at a time and required a crane to unload. The 140 lb. (63.50 kg) galvanized steel centerboards were packed separately and, while being unloaded, one fell on my feet. Luckily, I was wearing boots, but was rushed to the old General Hospital, anyway. My boots and socks were pierced yet the x-ray showed my blue-black-red-green feet were neither crushed nor broken. I once remember a surgeon who drilled my sinuses, complaining bitterly that my bones were as hard as steel. Well, he was proved right!

Fred and Audrey playing with their Waterskate kayaks

Life in the Sailboat World

I was really upset to learn later that this fine company went bankrupt—probably another banker nervous about the boat business in a downturn. Trouble can happen to anyone.

After the Toronto show one year, we left a provisionally sold 15 ft. (4.57 m) Commodore in the care of an Oakville trucking company. We checked regularly, but no sale materialized, so we planned to pick it up for another show. I arrived with trailer and was told the boat had been stolen, but not reported to the police. I smelled a rat and as I was leaving, someone whispered the Commodore was with so and so in Brampton! I drove there immediately, and there she was, hidden in long grass.

I decided a commando raid was needed and knew just the fellow to pull it off. He was a long retired commander of a Dutch cruiser that had sunk two Japanese submarines. He had been

Cocooning the boats for winter delivery. Fred fell from the top of this trailer at the Regina Boat Show.

Life in the Sailboat World

required to fight against the Indonesian freedom soldiers and he told me he had to machine gun from a mound of fallen men. Somehow, he managed to join the allied invasion fleet at Normandy. Bob Roffel was wonderful help at the Toronto Boat Show and he jumped at another foray into danger and liberation! We drove to Brampton and found our boat, neglected and laying forlornly between a bunch of power boats. We loaded in less than five minutes and took off like a bat out of hell being chased by someone screaming we couldn't do that. We said "watch us," but I doubt that he heard.

We were thrilled to have sold eight pedal boats to a town north of Edmonton. They were carefully loaded, and I took off in my Comanche truck in low winter clouds. I rarely drove over 55 mph. (90 km/h) with loads, but got the surprise of my life when I saw in my rear mirror that my huge tandem trailer was swinging round to shake my hand. I realized in a flash that I was on black ice and steered like crazy to straighten out. But the trailer was not finished with me and swung wildly to the passenger front window and snapped off the hitch. Out of the corner of my eye, I saw the load hit the ditch, unbelievably roll over 360 degrees and come to a stop.

The RCMP drove up and said many other vehicles were off the road. A tow truck eventually came, a real professional, who pulled the trailer upright out of the ditch. A few upright posts had crumbled and wiring was torn out, but only two paddle wheel blades were broken. The damage was so minimal, I decided to drive on and deliver the load. The wonderful customer almost embraced me, took the load as if nothing had happened, and presented me with a cheque. Needless to say we got him some paddle wheel blades on the double and once again realized the value of careful loading and continually checking the tie downs.

Life in the Sailboat World

The Sailing Game

Life in the Sailboat World

Chapter 6

Building Sailboats

Boat Building

As in any business, labour constantly needs attention. Besides wages, one is dealing with holidays, time off, dress, hygiene, work ethic, and attitudes. The company motto was Customers Make Paydays Possible, and we worked at getting employees to see the connection. We watched performance on the job, accuracy in the shop, and in administration. I am sad to say that many were ill-prepared by their education and upbringing. We taught a lot of basics that should have been learned earlier.

Boats have to be crafted to incredible precision. A deck has to be lowered exactly into position on a hull, and you have no idea how many went on crooked. Centerboard slots have to be centred, and parts like gudgeons, shroud-anchor plates, fairlead tracks, mainsheet blocks, and deck plates have to be at precise locations. Building a mast and boom demands an exactitude that requires the patience of one in love with the craft itself.

Building catamarans merely doubles the accuracy headache. In time, we achieved a high standard of about 1/16 in. (2mm) over a 15-foot length (4.5 m), and some RCAF officers told us they wished their jet fighters were built with such precision.

I often thought the main reason we beat the Americans time and time again in the Sea Spray Championships was, besides the skipper, the perfect line up of the hulls. Even the designer Allan Arnold ended up taking a Sea Spray from us in lieu of the final franchise payment.

Installing the work ethic was a task of a different sort and required care and concentration. Iron-handed leadership was

A nest of Sea Spray sailors in Osoyoos, British Columbia. Dave West, centre, won the championship ten times.

required to have product delivered on time and built to the highest standards. In the seventies and eighties, there were no courses teaching boat builders the tricks of the trade in fibreglass, concrete, wood, and aluminum. I was pleased to see in the nineties that the government has a job classification for both building and fitting out boats. Water-tight hulls are another acquired art, especially as finding leaks is time consuming. Once a boat is built, sold, and shipped, you don't want to see it again.

We always tried to maintain a high building standard and bent over backwards if ever a problem arose. I remember an Ontario customer claiming his Kolibri 2-12 had developed blisters. This was a new problem, so we took his word and shipped him another hull under warranty. When the faulty hull arrived back in our yard, we could see it had developed osmosis from being moored in an acidic lake and was not warrantable. One learns all the time, and now permanent lake moorage is in most warranty exclusions. There are now isothalic resins which fight the acid-rain polluted lakes.

I once delivered a Sea Spray to a Saskatchewan farmer, and a week later he complained that one hull leaked badly. Again, we replaced the boat, but on close inspection, I found a tree branch piercing the inside of the daggerboard box. We let him keep the new boat, but his wife later admitted his charade and apologized for his lack of forthrightness.

At the other end of the spectrum, we often received dealer boats with leaks or major shortcomings. Such deficiencies cost us valuable factory space and time, but I never blamed their workers as I felt management has the ultimate responsibility to supervise and test the boats sold. Input is required from beginning to end.

We approached Bombardier's marine division to build their sailboats under license. They had good looking, well performing boats, but they were built to poor standards. We tried twice, but never received an acknowledgment. After a few years, Bombardier dropped sailboats and sold the division to an insignificant outfit in central Ontario. We felt our trained workers could have produced their models by the hundreds on a royalty basis just like the Sea Spray and Enterprise.

Creating the Kolibri 2-12 Dinghy

When we started to make our version of this fine little sailboat in 1979 we made a few changes. We kept the same hull and deck design, mast and boom lengths, sail area and insignia. We replaced the troublesome daggerboard with a pivoting centre board and got rid of the double hull construction. We used 1/16 in. (2mm) Coremat from the Netherlands to make a sandwich construction hull that was super strong. We installed heavier and stronger gudgeons and rudder assembly, and introduced more sophisticated fittings and heavier sails. In a few moves, we considerably updated the Kolibri, which we now made out of fibreglass instead of injection molded plastic.

We switched to 2-component urethane foam guaranteed not to absorb water, but down the road found that this so-called wonder product took on water. We switched again to polyethylene air bags, which it is claimed will outlast the boat!

The moment of truth arrived. In November 1979, I took the prototype Kolibri 2-12 on my Jeep and headed for Naramata, near Penticton, where the lake was still open. I stayed with longtime friends and fellow Sea Spray sailors John and Angela Harrop, who helped rig and get the new baby into the water. We poured beer over the fore deck and launched into a moderate wind. I sailed her through her paces and last, but

The classic Kolibri 2-12, a large part of Glenmore's history

not least, did a capsize test, relieved to find our new mahogany laminated centerboard did not snap. All went well, and I smelled we had a winner on our hands. Even though I had worn a wetsuit, the Harrops' garden sauna was marvelous as I rolled back and forth through the snow getting my blood running, chuckling all the time about our new Kolibri, which was to become the mainstay of our boat line up.

The Harrops were an interesting

The classic Kolibri 2-12 with too many people on board

couple: he was a professor and she a short wave radio operator. She had joined the coast guard, and did a yearly tour of duty in Innuvik in the Arctic. Both raced; in light/moderate winds Angela used to beat the pants off us Sea Spray sailors. She also ocean sailed legs of a round-the-world trip with relatives, bringing a 40-footer (12 m) through the Panama Canal.

Flotation Problems

In the beginning, we bought two component A+B closed cell urethane floatation; it was coast guard approved and took on only 5% of its weight after being submerged 24 hours.

By the early nineties, we found this claim to be untrue and encountered numerous water-logged boats. The interior foam was often so swollen the hulls looked like washboard and there was an enormous weight increase. Other manufacturers were experiencing the same problem, and only boats well protected in winter seemed to escape. We frequently removed sodden foam, decreased boat weight 30 to 50 lbs. (13.6 kg to 22.7 kg), and installed PVC floatation air bags.

We tried to get the foam suppliers to take responsibility, but as usual the big guys have their guns loaded with excuses: we did not mix right; we did not pour at the right temperature; we subjected the containers to frost. Who knows, maybe they froze on the way to us! All material for a class action, but not affordable by a small boat company. Boats could lose their vital flotation and sink, and owners faced the cost of removing the sodden foam or living with misshapen boats.

Removing this wet, smelly foam was a dirty and difficult job at the best of times and extremely labour intensive. Steel rods were needed to loosen the leeched in foam from the fibreglass. Workers had to wear masks to protect against the gasses emitted. And there was the continual worry of piercing the hull. Defoaming could cost as much as $1,000, but we managed to get costs down over time to about $350. These are substantial figures to put against low priced boats.

Since 1990 we have used only PVC air bags to provide flotation and find they do their job year after year, causing no condensation. Laser was smart enough to use this system right from the seventies. Although Styrofoam had a reputation for taking on water, if placed above water level it, too, does an adequate flotation job.

Other Tests (or Heart Attacks)

I can remember at least seven product tests that gave us sleepless nights. Allan Arnold, the Sea Spray designer, was anxious for us to sell his Sesame and Kimba Kat. Sesame had a fair amount of sail for a little flat-bottomed dinghy, but Duuk tried her out in a strong breeze and reported she was fast but erratic. The only way he could stop capsizing was to sail a wavy course, so Sesame would be no good for the general public. We sold the four in stock, and that was that. Its copy, the Arrow, had numerous problems too, and we never took one on trade or consignment.

I still remember the catty remarks we got from onlookers as we beat a hasty retreat to shore when a pedal boat we were testing sank. A small hole was found to be the cause. We sent a long report to Future Beach about the shipwreck, and the four-seater was immediately replaced and never gave any more trouble. We had almost as much fun testing the original two-seater. After a morning of spring skiing at Panorama, we put the boat in at lake's edge where the ice was beginning to melt. It was our first real understanding of what "enormous freeboard" meant. We would have been soaked in any other pedal boat, but with Golden Goose, as we named her, our ski suits stayed as dry as toast. We didn't realize how many cottagers had been spying on our cold, strange endeavour until the summer when they dropped by the store and told us.

One tries to do tests in quiet spots where a crowd can't witness any failures. Typically, the public does not realize most new products go through development curves. Future Beach claimed their

Allan Arnold, Sea Spray designer and aerospace engineer, also loved planes

highly touted outrigger Barracuda water bike had been through every test in the book. It struck me as a manual Sea-doo and would appeal to the health nut and the anti-noise pollution crowd.

Prairie winters make westerners anxious to get back on the water. The Calgary Yacht Club had just reopened for the season and seemed the ideal place to do our test. I eased her into the water and immediately felt her instability, so headed back to the dock, but in a quick flash, I capsized and inverted her in full view of all the Club members. We let children try her later and, because they are lighter and have a lower centre of gravity, they did just fine.

Yet another report went to Future Beach, and improved versions appeared. One couple on one of Calgary's millionaire lakes fell in love with Barracuda, but it still had problems, so we offered a refund. What should have been sales coup fell flat, but it ended well when this charming couple tried Hobie's brand new Mirage pedaling kayak. Another success story began.

We very much believed in the Barracuda concept. Future Beach had spent millions on development, and we know it will be sorted out soon.

We tried very hard to get city sailing school business and demonstrated a Spindrift made in Ontario. During the capsize display our skipper just couldn't right her. Boat tests are full of broken dreams!

Chapter 7

Boatbuilding Bigwigs

A Pillar in the Dinghy Industry
Steve Clark, Laser Builder

After a few emails and phone calls across the continent, we met at the Amtrak train station at Providence, Rhode Island. I thought only a man with good qualities would take time out to meet total strangers, even if we had been a Laser dealer for some years.

The factory was at Portsmouth, but first Steve drove us around the beautiful corner of Rhode Island, which harbours the cottage-mansions of Newport Beach. It was March and a gloriously windy, blustery, dark snowy Atlantic day. Gigantic waves rolled in and were a dramatic back drop to these still beautiful symbols of bygone wealth.

The rest of the day he showed us a modern, efficient American small boat plant, where even the boxing was mechanized. We regretted not having seen the plant earlier to have a deeper understanding of what happened when we ordered a boat. Steve told us he retrieved the Little America Cup from the Aussies in 1996 after a four-year campaign; while the world didn't give them much recognition, I certainly offered a belated three cheers! Steve also raced International Canoes and A-Class Catamarans so we had a long catamaran background in common. Vanguard is a fine quality builder in this age of mediocrity, and I wished him and his associates continued success and fair winds. I found it an outstanding visit.

When did you join Vanguard?

As entrepreneurs we set up our on shop in upstate New York

Steve Clark, Laser Builder

in 1977 and started professionally building boats. We proceeded through various incarnations of that and moved to Rhode Island in 1981. We took a big step in winter 1986 and bought Vanguard from the Harken brothers. I recruited Chip Jones, a ten-year-younger friend, to form a partnership to run Vanguard, and we moved the Wisconsin factory to Rhode Island.

Are any board members actively involved in management?

Strictly speaking there are two stockholders: Chip and me, and we are both directly involved 100% in management. We retain two consultants to work with us perhaps as "paid members of the board" who provide expertise. One of them is retired with a manufacturing background, and the other has very good financial and human resource skills. We use their expertise all the time and they challenge our thinking at our monthly board meetings.

What was your background or did you go straight into boatbuilding?

I tried teaching after graduate school, but did not succeed at it. I went out to the back yard and started building boats again, so you might say a small business background. Additionally, my father had been operating a sort of one-man venture capital fund for a number of years, and when he died, I had to evaluate these closely held companies and liquidate or sell them. This function of closing my father's estate gave me high-wire training in essential business valuation, and buying and selling businesses. So this was my immediate background before buying Vanguard, although I had also acquired successful positions in a number of significant companies.

Life in the Sailboat World

And obviously Vanguard appears successful.

We try to be and sometimes we are more successful than other times. Chip became product line manager at Sippican Ocean Systems, a company my father had started, so while he had an engineering background, he was basically working in submarine warfare systems. He acquired a very strong business, product management, and manufacturing background. We have complimented each other's abilities quite well, and I attribute a great deal of Vanguard's success to Chip's efforts.

It is remarkable that business people are often the better engineers and vice versa. It goes back and forth, but Chip has been the Chief Executive Officer for the last 10 to 12 years. He is currently taking a six-month sabbatical, cruising the Caribbean just to refresh his vision and get some warmth.

It is sometimes needed in business.

Yes, it has been a goal or dream of his for years. He found a C&C sailboat needing lots of work and he personally refurbished it over a three-year period and, this winter, got to go. I feel it's great. I, too, have run away periodically and believe it a good thing, if one's work can support it. Sometimes you believe an organization can't survive without you. It takes a lot of maturity, and you need to impart to your staff they are perfectly capable of taking over the job you ask of them and will pay them well. It is totally possible for staff to meet, make sound decisions, and carry on!

We run a very open company with few financial secrets. At our month end closing meetings, senior management discusses financial performance, tracks budgets, and a bunch of other things. We did this from the start when we were much smaller; we were thought odd and criticized for spending so much time on financial tracking and management. Our aim was to have everyone on the same page, pulling the same oar, and know absolutely where we stood.

Glenmore boats too always followed monthly control procedures.

The recent 9/11 disaster brought home the value of this type of financial control. We were able to assess quickly what our situation would be, based on fourth quarter estimates not being achieved. The outcome was [that] even with strong fall programmes, we would not achieve our goals, so we aggressively cut costs and production and got overhead and overtime down to zero. We culled a lot of manufacturing dead wood, less than satisfactory employees were laid off, and we didn't replace retiring clerical, advertising, and office staff. We confidently made the course correction and didn't hit the ground very hard. We were able to tell where we were going and what to do about it.

Did you say you made even deeper fall and winter promotions?

We went one step further. In October, sales were really lagging, so we stepped up to the plate and went into further discounting to re-stimulate those sales.

Glenmore boats benefited from those deep promotions and doubled sales in the last quarter.

It is funny [how] something like that happens in tough times. A lot of proactive, strong, and positive people are fine in the good years, but there are those waiting for the sky to fall. Things can get worse and who knows what can come down; then I guess, it's a question of organizational optimism. In the same environment you see consumer confidence can stay very strong; certainly the automotive industry has poured lot of product into the market, although I suspect they paid a great deal to do it. Zero percent financing is going to haunt them for a long time.

Profits were down but they moved product.

You have the situation that you must preserve cash and not build inventory that soon becomes obsolete inventory. You must pull back and be positioned to make money in the future. If you are stranded behind a big buffer of obsolete inventory, it will not be possible to make money in the near term. The other side of the coin is that if the auto industry didn't make any inventory, there would be no cars for people to get off the fence and buy.

Glenmore went positive with the slogan "afraid of flying – go sailing." Over the last ten years, have unit sales increased each year or has it been a wavy line?

Pretty much a good sales curve, sometimes not achieving what we had budgeted, but have managed to grow sales. During the last ten years, we have also grown the company by acquisition. Five years ago we acquired the Sunfish and Laser brands from SLI Inc. and rolled these assets into Vanguard. That created a huge spike in sales, something like $5 to $6 million. You pay a lot of money and you cannot forget you have to finance this huge debt. This year we added Seitech dollies. So we have grown not only in product line, but by new acquisition. We operate Seitech separately, but at the end of the day it consolidates into one bottom line.

You always used Seitech in promotions, so it must work well as a subsidiary?

Yes, for some five years and it has helped dealers give consumers free gear.

Did Olympic status widely increase laser sales and what about the 470 and 49er?

The Olympic Classes we have built over the years are the Finn and Europe, 470, Laser and the 49er. In terms of money, we were very successful with the Finn business, being the Olympic Finn supplier until we dropped it from our line. We conceded

The Olympic Laser in tight competition
Photo Courtesy of Vanguard Sailboats Inc.

Life in the Sailboat World

the business to Lemieux and Devoti after we built 50 Finns for the Barcelona Games. At that point we felt we had played the Finn card.

We had a good run of about 40 to 50 Europe dinghies, and then word came back that our hull shape was wrong. We really don't know how that happened, since we pretty well exactly copied a fast hull shape. We then fared up a minutely modified winning hull form, but somehow the Class became convinced our boat was unsailable downwind in heavy air. Given the modifications we made, it didn't make a lot of sense. At the same time, the Swedish builder Finnessa went back into manufacturing, making fairly significant hull changes to straighten out the buttocks along with other improvements. So, probably Finnessa ended up the better boat. We didn't have the resources or in Swedish "the ork" to destroy an essentially brand new set of molds and retool to stay in the Europe business. So, we didn't hang very well building the Europe.

We had a sort of a checkered time with the 470. We built both very good boats and some not so good. The 49er we bring in from New Zealand.

Although it does not apply to Laser, the problem with Olympic classes, generally speaking, is that serious people are really working hard and getting a lot better than run of the mill sailors. Such enthusiasts form their own elite group and basically drive out the weekend warriors or more casual racers.

In the US we see, with the Europe, 470, and 49er, new classes, a great rush of enthusiasm over the two or three years leading up to the Olympics, then the teams break up. They get disenchanted with training as hard as they have to, become burned out, and find they have spent more money than they should have. The next generation teams find the numbers down significantly from the first campaigns. Women's 470 went from 18 teams in the 1988 trials to about 3 at the 1992 trials. The bottom fell out of the earlier efforts; the winners take home their trophies and the class just stops.

The Laser Class fortunately appears strong, with different

generations sailing in a variety of fleets such as Masters, juniors, the Women's, and the Radials. There are enough different constituencies within the Laser Class to enable people to get over the fact that the top half of the fleet is full of people taking it very much more seriously than the rest of us. Top halfers will not be nice to you at the weather mark, because it means a whole lot more to them. They really work harder at it than everyone else and will do better. In fact, they believe themselves they deserve to do better, and you don't have the right to be on the race course with them. The lower half doesn't have the time or will to commit to training and are quite put off when the top guys are nasty to them.

You can always prove that working harder is better than not working harder; that people who sail and train more increase significantly the probability of beating you. If you don't realize this, you should stop competing. You must accept that if you are in a top ten finish or even top half finish you are lucky, and the more you push, the top half of the table suddenly gets a lot hungrier. It's very different noodling around in the top ten thinking your pretty good, than noodling around the bottom third where the other guys are probably at your level and pushing each other. You tend to forget there are a whole lot ahead of you. It's what happens when standards go up, but the standards don't raise all boats.

I think one of the things that make Lasers work as an Olympic class is that it is a big enough business, we don't know whose boat we are building. Moreover, the plant and whole distribution system is shuffled around enough that customers can believe we are doing a good job producing consistent boats, so they don't go looking for magic or try to make us build their magic. So, the third Laser I built this morning could be for the number one Canadian contender. I should know, but I don't. I am trying to say the best sailor in the world could be getting the third boat we built today, nobody knows.

With the 470, I always knew whose boat I was building. Oh, my gosh, this boat is for Tom Kinney and it has to be perfect, or this boat is for Pease and Cindy and it better be right.

Life in the Sailboat World

With the 49er, we always had the name attached. The customer knew which boat was theirs and when we were building it. The process was much more personal and made the customer's investment in the boat a very different deal. A Laser is bought off the rack, making it possible to inventory and distribute boats efficiently, but other classes lack the volume to make this practical.

The last batch of boats we did for the Barcelona Olympics was a huge deal, and we had to sell off 60 Finns after the event, which we managed to do. Actually, the way we made money was not on the sale of boats, but on the advance deposits from Barcelona which allowed us to not use our line of credit. We were much more profitable prior to the Olympics and, in fact, our annual profits came from the deposit, not the proceeds of the huge boat order, which were negligible.

Glenmore Boats had similar experiences with government order progress advances. I predicted to David Dilman, then our Vanguard rep, that boat builders would set up factory stores. He was surprised, but I see you operate a store in California and right here by the plant.

We started the store next door because our local dealer was fairly pathetic. People came to the factory wanting a Sunfish rudder, and we were forced to say we can't sell you one and send him to the dealer, knowing full well he didn't have one in stock. The dealer would tell the customer he could have the rudder that afternoon and rush over here to pick it up.

We were so tempted to tell a customer take the part to the dealer and have him take your money because, as the builder, we can't sell direct. The issue was we simply had to do a better job supporting customers in our own backyard, and eventually opened our on-site Boat Locker in partnership with another dealer.

The Southern California Sailing Centre is a case of where we thought a critical market was being poorly serviced by existing dealers. We took the opportunity to improve the situation and meet the very specific needs of the California college market, which insists we have Flying Juniors in stock to satisfy our contract with them. We needed a means to inventory boats on the West Coast and avoid a full dealer markup, as there is insufficient margin in college boat sales.

So, southern California is a somewhat special circumstance where area dealers were under performing and not meeting the special obligations of most important customers. We are learning all the time about these troubling aspects.

You may know Vanguard, prior to acquiring Sunfish Laser Inc., was a direct marketing company here in Rhode Island. One of the major benefits in acquiring Sunfish Laser was, we got a distribution network with enough volume to make shipping boats around the country cost effective. Two mainline Vanguard products, our 15 and Club 420, have grown dramatically because of nation-wide distribution.

During a rough economic period, to survive, Glenmore switched to a mixture of direct sales and dealers. Vanguard reserves the right to handle institutional sales where low margins are imperative. We dealers want these sales. Even though groups perceive they get rock bottom prices dealing with the factory. What can we do to solve these issues?

Yes, there is an issue and I believe we are ready to discuss special pricing that will satisfy the buyer and any dealer who feels he can put together an institutional sale. Typically, we do not want to put dealers in the middle of the scholastic and college market where we have a hard time. Those guys get prices at a level where there is nothing for anybody else, but it is the nature of that particular market. Whether, in the long term, this market will change is unknown. You have to remember they want boats significantly different from off the shelf models, and this means higher costs to weigh against the margins.

We have discussed day to day problems in boat manufacturing, but what are the strategic problems?

One of the biggest problems affecting growth of the sport and markets is access; that is, access to water, the ability to leave your boat/trailer some place so that sailing is not a four-hour operation every time. One of the reasons we like our dolly business so much is that a dolly enables you to get a boat in and out of the water quickly. Today's waterfront real estate values make it impossible for private individuals to band together and form a club like in the old days. With public parks there is a huge issue of working out the needs of the sport of sailing versus other sports. It is almost a vicious circle where so few sail, but unless people have access to sailing in a public area, how will more people get acquainted with sailing.

There are other issues regarding the knowledge transfer: how boats get bought and sold, how people get trained to sail. I have been impressed recently by the success of the kayak market, where the sport is basically, fundamentally, stupidly easy. The industry has offered a great deal of training and support in the use of the product after you have bought a kayak. There are a lot more guided tours and down river paddling trips, so an industry not big in dollars is out there consistently helping to perfect your use of the product.

You buy a sailboat, take a few lessons, and then are thrown out into the world on your own. Unless you are in a racing group, there is very little support for you down the road. There are very few cruising clubs; so, the only organized constituency for you is to race your boat where you need a competitive skill base. Few want to race and a void arises that drives participation away from sailing, rather than increasing it.

The City of Calgary should be congratulated for providing an easily accessed sailing school and economical boat parking. A high percentage of Calgarians sail as a result, and life in Calgary would have been a lot less pleasant without its sailing factor.

That is it exactly; the problem of where to put your boat and get on the water quickly was solved.

These days if it isn't quick, quick, quick, a kid doesn't want to do it.

Where do you park your boat if you live in an apartment block

Life in the Sailboat World

or condominium? A whole lot of baggage seems to come with sailing. Just think what a pain in the arse an automobile is in the city, and now you are adding a boat to that? What options do you have that don't cost thousands of dollars? In my part of the world, you can belong to a suburban yacht club, drive 40 minutes to get to your boat and that solution costs $600 to $700 a year.

Is that too much for a lot of people?

If all the clubs are full and not accepting new members, cost doesn't matter. Every yachting club in this area has a waiting list, so even if you paid the $1,000 entry fee and $700 annual fee to park your boat there, it doesn't do you any good because of the waiting period.

There is an urgent need for more clubs, but no real estate to do it. Waterfront land large enough for a club site is scarce and assumes you can get a club variance past the zoning board. It would cost you a number starting with two followed by six zeros. You would have to assemble a group of extraordinarily wealthy people willing to pony up a lot of money to start something. And at the end of it all, will this help a 19-year-old college kid with a Laser, for whom thirty bucks a month is a lot of money?

You mentioned college support.

Well, there are inter scholastic/collegiate sailing programmes, but it receives the same amount of support as any other collegiate sport. Cornell University Sailing Team has a fleet of boats, but their annual operating budget comes from the student life allocation handed out by the student senate. They are lucky if they get $2,500 to finance their Spring Programme, which doesn't buy a lot of gasoline or hotel rooms. They have a place on Cayuda Lake to keep their boats and can get transportation and entry fee support, but they can't afford a coach.

It's easy for sailing to fall into the elitist trap.

The people who can afford to play, play. It was very forward thinking of the City of Calgary forty years ago to own boats and offer parking.

There is a small community based sailing programme in

Providence, as well as long standing community sailing programmes in Boston and elsewhere. They are popping up and there is a strong movement to get new people into the sport. But how do they stay there and take the next step? The next step is you paid $50 for a good community programme, moved to the suburbs, and found you have to belong to an exclusive club which has a $1,500 initiation fee. There is a big gap between the cup and the lip.

No wonder people take up kite-flying.

Or surfing. Anything where you can whip up to the parking lot, pull your gear off the car top, and have action in ten minutes is pretty cool. Even with kite sailing the kits are expensive, about $1,700 in Canada. It seems like a lot of dough to be dragged around on your stomach while learning, and I feel there are risks and you can get into bad trouble in a big hurry. You can end up a long way from the beach, surrounded by a lot of expensive stuff in the water with no way to get home. On a wind surfer, at least, you can ditch the rig, float your belly on the board, and paddle in. With a kite, all you have is a wake board, so it is a long swim if you run into trouble two miles from the beach. You can go twenty miles down wind very quickly. Then, there is the insurance liability problem.

It had been an hour's drive through excruciatingly heavy rain. I thanked Steve for his generous time allotment and was impressed with the erudite view of his company, the industry and sailing.

The Incredible Success Story of Hobie Catamarans.

I met with Hobie in the San Juans on his fantastic 60 ft. (18.2 m) catamaran powerboat moored at the bottom of the beach. He and his wife were living on board while rebuilding their cottage. I told him Hobie Cats had always been just below my level of consciousness and that a close friend still sails one of the first 14s sold in Canada. My intention was to write about the dynamic, worldwide Hobie sailboat success, and his part in tempting thousand of people into the joys of sailing.

Part 1 Growing up and early surfboard days

Hobie looked to be in his late fifties, fit and full of life, but admitted to being in his late sixties. He had grown up in California on his father's orange grove.

I had heard in the 1960s that he was home-building sail boards better than anything on the market, and he was quick to tell me he built surfboards, never sail boards. In fact, he had built a board for his friend, Hoyle Schweitzer, the Windsurfer originator, who started around the same time he began his catamarans. Hoyle brought him a Windsurfer to try, and, though a boarder and sailor, Hobie found it challenging to learn. It took a long time for windsurfing to get going, but eventually the Europeans got hot on them. Windsurfing came back to the States and took off, especially after the public accepted there was a learning curve.

He started working on the 14 in 1967, and it was out for sale a year later; the 16 was ready for sale in 1971. He had not studied engineering or design, but had taken mechanical drawing and math, and that his real skills came from hobbies and other home experiences.

Hobie Alter on board in the San Juans with his wife, Susan

Life in the Sailboat World

He had been building model airplanes since he was small, which he considered structural work. When he was 13, he made an outbuilding with studded walls, shingled roof, water and electricity, for which his Dad agreed to pay, if he did it right. It was 10 ft. by 6 ft. (3m by 2m) and was his own space for a photography darkroom and other hobbies, like kite building.

He was involved with the passions of his time, like surf boarding, and for about four years, he was building surfboards in his folk's garage. There was no real industry at the time; he was still in high school and then junior college, and they were just a bunch of guys making boards in their garages. If a glue press was needed, they just came up with something to improve the clamping. Then a shaping machine was needed, and Hobie thought up a unit that had rails and curved lengthwise and crosswise. He ran constants over a balsa block to get closer to shape, and then continued hand shaping. He was intent on improving the method of fixing a fin to a surfboard. It was pure trial and error, because with fibreglass, they needed to determine if more or less material was needed and where the weak spots were.

It was a seat-of-the-pants era, but in this surfing environment, he got to meet people who did have engineering backgrounds, who could steer him right, or introduce him to people who normally wouldn't speak to him. A lot that rubbed off from surfing customers went into the boards.

I wondered if he had business experience helping his dad in the orange grove, and he said no, except that one year his parents wanted to travel. He had been helping his father smudge oranges at $1.00 an hour. Smudging was a system to keep the oranges from freezing; oil sat in containers between the rows and gave off heat when lit. People were hired especially to light the oil, and his father offered him 50% of any saving he made looking after the smudging operation in his absence. Dad was a thrifty fellow and watched the hourly oil costs. He would light only the rows where heat was needed and watched the temperature at different times of night. Hobie absorbed all this frugality and saved $3,000 during the trip; his father let him keep it all — a lot of money in those days.

The family lived a conservative life and had many good things, but Hobie couldn't call them big spenders. They were generous with him and his sister, and they, in turn, were obliged to look after their toys. They were given most things they wanted, but it would always be a Chevy rather than a Cadillac.

So his business experience really came through building the boards for himself and his friends. He took bookings each summer and was able to produce about twenty. He told me he soon learned that it cost $X for resin, balsa wood, and glass, and although the garage was rent free and his labour thrown in, he only made about $20 a board. He later thought a lot more about overhead and taxes and learned he couldn't do it all himself. He started hiring and training friends to help as the boards got more popular, but Hobie continued to do all the shaping. Nobody had much experience; it wasn't even an industry yet, but he kept picking up tips and learning what he could.

The first catamarans around were Woody Brown's Beach Cats in Hawaii, 40 feet (12 m) long, with asymmetric hulls, and built for tourist rides in Waikiki. Woody and his friends were surfers, too, and gave Hobie his first taste of catamaran sailing. Meanwhile, a few of Hobie's friends were making outriggers and they were the first multihulls to hit the California coast.

Warren Seaman manufactured a few outriggers and put out a set of plans for home building. Hobie tried to assemble his own outrigger, but was so busy with his surfboard business, he gave it to a friend to finish, on the promise he could borrow it. He crewed for friends occasionally, but still hadn't really learned to sail.

His first real taste of cat sailing was when he crewed for his friend, Phil Edwards, in the Ensenada race. Hobie then bought a used P-Cat, and although it needed a few guys to carry it down the beach, he was soon riding the waves and flying hulls. Although not seriously involved, he was intrigued watching his friend Carter Pile develop and sell P-Cats.

Part 2 Developing the famous Hobie Catamarans

Phil Edwards and Sandy Banks, two of Hobie's surfboard shaping employees, built an 11 ft. (4 m) cat out of surfboard blanks. It was light enough for one guy to run it down the beach and launch it through the surf. Basically this model, which had no daggerboards, was too small and very sensitive to tipping over in all directions, but it did bring out the fact that a small boat could work and be a fun product at the same time. Some ten years earlier, Phil had built his own 20 ft. (6.8 m) El Gato catamaran with a huge sail; it was something like a Tornado cat, which came much later in 1967.

Hobie had been subconsciously watching catamaran development; one day a fellow came by looking to buy his surfboard company, accompanied by a business friend, sent by the fellow's mother. None too seriously, Hobie put a really big figure on the table. They asked him what else he could do, and he suggested there was room for a good small 12 ft.-14 ft. (3.7 m to 4.3 m) catamaran, light enough to be dragged down a beach by one guy. Hobie said if he had the time, he would like to explore such a catamaran. No more was said, and he thought they were not interested in buying the surfboard operation.

About a month later, the business advisor, Art Hendrickson, returned, saying his friend didn't want the board business, but he thought the small catamaran sounded interesting. He asked Hobie if he would like to concentrate on building and testing such a cat, while he took care of running the business.

They agreed to each put $5,000 in the bank; Hobie cleared out his motor cycles from an old Quonset hut near his board shop and got to work.

He told Art they should use the impressive little Cal Cat as a trial horse, even though it had daggerboards. They purchased one and then a second to use the rigging on the Hobie prototype to get fair comparisons. They saw immediately a cat without daggerboards presented a whole new set of problems. They found that the width in relation to the length needed to be narrower as the boat got longer. The boat had to sit deep enough in the water to prevent side slippage, and a hull with a flatter outer side sat deeper in the water and acheived lateral resistance.

They found within a few minutes of testing they could tell what a prototype could do, whether good or bad, and were able to move on to the next prototype very fast. There were no marine chandleries at the time, and initially they used simplistic hardware grade fittings.

It took a week to build a new set of hulls, and they went through three prototypes, each one evolving into what they were looking for and light enough for one to drag down the beach. Not being a sophisticated sailor, his goal was a simple, efficient rig to steer and sheet, go in and out of the surf, and ride waves.

So while all this testing was fun, his partner, as a non-sailor, was getting nervous. Hobie decided they had to get moving and produce something.

He was confident the prototype was performing well and that it would be worthwhile producing as a first class commercial model. He felt it was a step forward over other cats then in the marketplace, and they decided to go ahead. In nine months they did all the tooling for the molds and castings.

They had to figure out how to raise the platform and started looking at aluminium casting pylons, and other connecting castings. His partner, Art, was a great help and would drive miles asking questions and sniffing out their needs. He ended up with a tremendous knowledge of the aluminium casting business.

Hobie used this fast education to make the plugs from which to take the patterns for the sand castings. The first rough set worked, and an experienced metal worker helped him grind, sculpt, and clean up the aluminum molds on the first go round so that they fit perfectly to the boat. Hobie learned from the metal worker and was able to produce all the castings, even though the approach was a bit Mickey Mouse.

He was able to convert a glue press from his surfboard operation to produce tubular bent crossbars, which avoided the plumbing look of other catamarans. They threaded the trampoline into the sail track and it integrated well with the front cross bar.

Then they went to local sail makers for the sail design and, in particular, Don McKibben. Even though the sail people were not catamaran guys, Hobie already had a feel for what he wanted. He would go out on the 14, test the sail, and find out if there was too much power up high or no luff control. He slowly learned what a cat sail was all about and brought it to near perfection.

Hobie believed he had reached his goal and that the 14 could easily sail off the beach, whether sea or lake, sat high enough out of the water, and had overcome problems other cats were encountering. He believed they had overbuilt the 14, but it would be hard to wreck, and the castings were strong enough for larger boats. In fact, when they moved on to the 16, they only needed to beef up a few little things and change the mast; the castings were identical and almost everything else was the same.

Everything was falling into place and about April 1968, the first complete prototype was out sailing, followed by the second and third models in May and June. They were nervous at only producing one boat a month, but by July 4 there were four models; they started up a production line.

I wondered why Hobie had used the asymmetric hull design; he said the idea came from the Woody's Beach Cat, although Woody's hulls were narrow in relation to the length. He found that a forty-foot boat cannot be reduced proportionately to fourteen feet—width has to be increased in relation to the length. He tried, with continual adjustments, to get the small hulls to do the same job as the Beach cat, which was to utilize the asymmetrical hull theory of giving lateral resistance in place of using daggerboards.

At a later date when attempting to scale up the 14 to the 16, they encountered the same proportional variance problems.

The Hobie 14 was not accepted right away. The established small boat dealers wanted nothing to do with catamarans. In

February, about seven months into production, they started exhibiting at boat shows. Art headed north and Hobie did the southern shows, and they fanned out across the country.

They quickly realized the key was to market first and then produce. They not only had to sell a boat—after all, there were other cats out there—but they also needed to convince the general public how much fun it could be to sail a little cat.

Bill Amberg, a friend of Hobie's, was working for the ski producer, Dick Barrymore, and had been filming the activities during the 14's development. He suggested Bill keep going and shoot a short continuous-wind 8 mm movie showing the 14 jumping and riding the waves as it went through the surf, flying hulls, tipping over, and the skipper having loads of fun.

The movie played continually at the shows and did indeed capture the imagination of a wider base of people, not necessarily sailors. A couple of guys would be walking through the show and their eye would catch all the crazy water antics of the little 14. They would declare their wives would kill them if they bought something like that, but lo and behold, they were back the next day to buy. There was no big money commitment at around $995.

And so sales began to flow. People would notice the crazy little boat out sailing, and this, too, generated sales.

Young people didn't mind capsizing—they were hungry for excitement. The first sales were not to established sailors, but to a bunch of ordinary guys like surfers, dirt bike riders, and skiers who were always looking for something exciting to do. A couple of fellows would be drinking beer, one would boast he was going to get one of those things, and the other wanted one, too. Not a bad way to get sales going.

Naturally some wanted to take girlfriends or wives, too, but Hobie felt the 14 was too small a boat for two people. Initially, they wanted to add a trapeze, but decided to keep it clean and safer. The 14 was such a light boat, she could come over on top of you pretty quickly.

The result was that Hobie was motivated to come out with a

two-person boat; namely, the 16. The 14 sold under the magic $1,000 figure at $995, and they worried that the 16 had to sell for more. After adding up the development costs, $1,700 turned out to be the figure.

Part 3 Production of the Hobie Catamarans

Production of the 14 was falling into place, and initially they worked with a few molds they moved around the room. Once production got up to ten a day, they incorporated a track on which to run the molds. It worked well, and oil in the track stopped resin build-up. Other boat manufacturers went with overhead track, but Hobie felt it was more complicated, and made the molds unstable when being worked on. While the molds moved along, they got waxed, gelcoated, layed up; and, for the first time in commercial boat production, sheets of urethane foam were vacuumed into place. A second lay-up was added, and then the hulls were popped and put in a finishing cycle after trimming. He was proud of the smooth little system they had set up.

I asked him if the 16 went as easily, and on the whole it did. They were able to use the same tracks, but did have a problem making the shroud attachment strong enough. First, they went to the side bar and into the hull, but were forced to go under the deck flange with a backing bar to get the strength. Doing the beefing up work properly took time. The dolphin striker and front cross bar went well, but a lot of time was required for the mast. They thought they could get away with putting diamond wire spreaders on the 14 extrusion, but these were a pain and did not work. His partner really wanted to use the 14 mast, but after wasting a lot of time, he convinced Art they had to build a new extrusion.

At that time, no one was extruding the thin-walled optimum masts the Hobie 16 needed. Now that the company was using a lot more aluminium, the extruders began listening, and they were able to get them to commit building thinner wall masts, following Hobie's design. They cam up with a pretty efficient product.

They were governed by the need for two people to be able to

right the boat from a capsize. Hobie told me the longer the mast, the more volume achieved, which resisted turtling (turning upside down) and made righting easier.

Another new idea was to put battens in the jib sail. They tried to avoid placing fairleads on the side bars, which would prevent sailors sliding up and down. They didn't want them on the trampoline either, as their idea was to keep the sailing comfortable and prevent injury from deck hazards every time one sailed. Placing the fairleads on the front cross bar was the ideal solution, but to get the right sheet lead, battens were needed in the jib. There was the drawback of the jib sheets catching the halyard at every tack, but they felt it the lesser evil.

So, production of the 16 also fell into place, the huge difference being that they had to manufacture a lot more 16s, and along with this came a need for more capital.

Hobie told me there were over 200,000 Hobies worldwide. He said although he worked on the 18, he was never a great fan, but they needed to protect their market from 18-footers (5.49 m) like the Nacra, which were coming out with daggerboards and straight hulls, claiming they would beat Hobies. Hobie 16s outsold all other classes every year right into the 21st century, and it looks like they have more winners on their hands with the rotationally molded Wave and Getaway. The 16 numbers are still high in France, Australia, and South Africa.

Part 4 Birth of the "Hobie Way of Life"

The 16 sold very fast, with many of the 14 guys trading up and the 14s bringing in a whole new bunch of sailors. Many retained their 14s along with the 16s. Sales were coming from all directions, and the Hobie owners started their own regatta system away from the yacht clubs with their stiffer environments, who didn't really want them and, furthermore, didn't have the space for them. The Hobie guys were a bit too obnoxious for the stiff yacht clubs and were not well enough schooled in the racing rules.

By the second year of the 16, they could easily get fifty Hobies at their southern California beach regattas; and fifty catamarans took up a lot of room! The habit of finding their own beach to put on a regatta spread across the States and Canada. They were acquiring more dealers, and the company taught them how to put on regattas and supported them with prizes and handouts.

Suddenly there were a lot of guys not only sailing well but racing, too, and the rules started smoothing out. Hobie always felt the clubs were stuffy, and the thought of having to retire after racing infractions really disgusted him. He equated it with football games not being over when fouls were made. So the Hobie group instituted the 360 degree turn for when sailors fouled the mark or another boat. This was a heavy penalty, but did not put you out of the running.

Hobie had read in a magazine that the Penguin class was experimenting with the same rule, but he felt they didn't need to experiment because it made all the sense in the world, and that was that. The 360 was in the Hobie rules almost the next day; everybody liked it, and it stopped people getting mad on the course. Despite more formality, the Hobie Regattas always put fun first!

It was often thought that Hobie sailors marched to a different drum; they shunned regular sailing clubs and just wanted to hang out together and have fun. Wherever there was a regatta, a campsite would be set up, preferably on the beach where everyone could see and participate in the activities. If a sailor preferred a hotel, he could be sure one was within sight. The campers all had one thing in common: they liked Hobie cats and didn't need outside entertainment. They sailed only so many

Nerve wracking moments as the Hobie 16s line up to start a race
Courtesy Hobieco

hours a day and spent the rest of the time partying, playing, and visiting. It all worked really well.

Hobie had, in fact, done this kind of socializing before, in his skiing days. They raced and then partied with the same group, and the same happened with he raced motor cycles in the desert. They would camp in the middle of the desert every weekend and have hare and hound races or scrambles with up to 500 guys in different classes. Friday nights, they would put out lime bags to mark some dirt road leading to nowhere and set up camp. Saturday, more campers showed up, and more socializing went along with the racing. So, these same models were used for the Hobie regattas, where sailors like to be on their own, not distracted by outside influences.

The Hobie Way of Life became part of the genre. There would be a "crash" class, which novices were encouraged to join, and then B and A Classes. Even if sailors were afraid to come out and try their hand, they encouraged them to participate for the fun. This attitude attracted more and more people, and whereas in surfing you don't want to be too crowded, with sailing, the aim was to get a good troop together. The regattas were strongly supported by the dealers and the Hobie Hotline magazine started and is still going strong.

I found it interesting to hear Hobie reflect that when the 14s and 16s were initially growing, there were not huge numbers at the beach regattas. It was easy for the company to organize the events and absorb the costs by allotting a certain percentage of sales—hamburgers for everyone! Over the next 35 years, the sales could not support the masses of boats participating. By this time, however, there were so many district fleets, they could and did run their own regattas very successfully. He felt very strongly that the class had done a great job in keeping the enthusiasm up for so many years. He said he still enjoys showing up at regattas and that the company support continues, but in a more general way.

Life in the Sailboat World

Part 5 Rotationally molded products – Hobie Hawks, Mirage Pedalling Kayaks, Float Cats, Waves, Getaways and Bravos

Hobie liked rotational molding, but felt it did better on certain products than others. It produces strong, inexpensive structures and is good for large pieces, but will never meet the high performance and light weight given by fibreglass structures.

In 1974, the Hobie Company produced over 10,000 injection molded nose cones for the Hobie Hawks. This was a futuristic, beautiful, radio controlled model glider, designed by Hobie. They used pre-pegged (pre-impregnated) epoxy and fibreglass to make the exceedingly light tail cone. While it was a perfect example of high strength-to-weight ratio, it proved unfeasible on a commercial basis. Just the same, it was a little marvel, its molded nose cone tough enough to use as a battering ram.

The Hobie Float Cat was the perfect product for rotary molding; it was easy to place inserts in the mold, which, when withdrawn, left perfect shapes to receive the cross tubes and other parts.

Hobie felt molded boats, being sealed products, were extremely hard to puncture, and were highly resistant to abrasion.

The Hobie kayaks were also rotary molded polyethylene and tough enough to drag up the beach. These came at a time when designers Greg and Dan Ketterman became Hobiecat shareholders. They added the trifoiler and the kayak lines, and most importantly, they developed the unique mirage drive kayak pedalling system. He thought the Kettermans added great design depth to Hobiecat, enhancing its future.

Rotary molding has been around a long time, but most early production was in trash cans and dumpsters. As it moved into the marine industry, the process, along with the tooling, became more refined.

We returned to talk of kayaks and I asked if Hobiecat had gone into an already crowded market place, just to spread their product line. He felt kayaks not only contributed to the direction the company was going, but came at a time when some catamaran sales were levelling out. I told him the Mirage pedaling kayak sold very well in Canada, even at a higher price; he felt the unique pedaling system was the huge attraction.

Legs are stronger than arms, so the pedaling kayaks are particularly good for the average non-professional kayaker. Once into competition, they prefer using paddles. He said there is nothing but good feedback on the Mirage, and sales continue to increase, especially now they have a version that is a bit shorter, completely set up for fishermen and quite different from the Float Cat. Hobie said he put a Mirage pedaling/steering mechanism on his Float Cat and was now able to go all over the place with it. He had kayaks on board his catamaran in the San Juans and told me they used them a lot. He said pedaling does not disturb perfectly glossy water, so you can see deep down.

Your legs are not in the water with the Mirage and, for him, it was the ideal fishing craft. He took his to gorgeous little Idaho lakes 7,000 ft. (2,000 m) up in the mountains with nobody around, and enjoyed the most sublime fishing experiences.

Part 6 Sailing and racing Hobies

The Hobie 16 got to be a very competitive boat, as simply rigged as it was, and even in the early days, it was common to see starting lines with over 30 hot-shot guys. Some liked to race the Hobie 18, too, when it came out. As time passed, even more sophisticated racing cats were added to the Hobiecat's stable, and now there is competitive racing in North America and other parts of the world, in 14s, 16s, 17s, 20s, FXIs and Tigers. Some of the rotomolded models are racing, too.

Hobie agreed one needed to know what one was doing on a 16, especially when driving it hard. He said with someone on the trapeze, you are really able to push her in heavy conditions. In early days, the Australians and Hawaiians sought out that kind of sailing, but now the rest of the world has the desire for the excitement of catamaraning.

Hobie found this demanding sailing element very interesting and remembered a time in Surfside, Texas, when he and his daughter, Paula, were racing in high Gulf winds. They reefed the main and got side by side with two of the hottest guys from Hawaii, the best heavy air sailors of the time. Paula and Hobie held up pretty good around the course and lost by only thirty seconds. He really loved sailing the 16, but his competitive days were dwindling.

He loved driving his 16 and did not consider it a particularly technical boat, with few adjustments to be made. It was just a matter of pushing, knowing the wind shifts, and planning ahead. He said you can't tack on every wind shift as with monohulls, so planning ahead to get into clean air is the way with catamarans.

He told me the 16 has produced some exceptional sailors, as has the Laser.

Part 7 The company moves on

While Art was neither sailor nor swimmer, he was good at raising capital and, for 10% of the company, they brought in a new guy who guaranteed a two-year $200,000 loan. Still, the growth raged and more capital was needed, so a small private offering was arranged.

In retrospect, Hobie wished the financing had stopped there, but his partner's interests were more on the business side of boating. Art had made wonderful contributions all along, but wanted them to become a public company, and that's what they did.

Hobie came to feel it had been a mistake; it was too costly, and being public meant a lot of outsiders were telling them how to do things. Still trying to grow the company, they found themselves at the mercy of people who did not know the boat business. Hobie would be outvoted in games played by the board. In one instance, the board wanted a 22 ft. to 23 ft. (6.7 m to 7.0 m) cat where you could live and sleep in the hulls. He tried to tell them all these things couldn't be done in that size, and, as it couldn't be easily trailered, they should forget the idea. Just the same, he attempted to make a small scale folding model, then a version with a cabin, neither of which made him happy.

I reminded Hobie that the Shark was a folding catamaran and

he agreed it worked, but noted it had insufficient room. He thought it was basically a good idea, but nobody had pushed it far enough yet.

He gave me another example of the irritations he was facing. By now, the Hobie board was largely comprised of non-boat people like lawyers, bankers, and stockbrokers, and he sat among them in his shirt sleeves. The board wanted him to talk to a guy they had hired to design a larger 25 ft. (7.62 m) catamaran; he had been involved with the Cigarette offshore racers. Hobie looked at the plans, which appeared to be a blow-up of the 16, but without attention to the proportional scaling requirement. The 23 ft. long, 18 in. wide and 24 in. high hulls were to contain captain's quarters, galley and a dining area. He saw immediately the hulls were too small, and the design could not work. He facetiously invited the designer to get under the 30 in. table, which measured 6 inches higher than the stateroom and galley!

The board had no inkling of what they were looking at in the impressive set of blue prints, and despite Hobie's misgivings, went ahead and paid $30,000 to have a prototype made in Florida.

Hobie felt life wasn't fun anymore; the board didn't like him, and probably the feeling was mutual. Around this time, the Coleman stove company renewed their interest in buying the company. Hobie didn't particularly want to sell, but he liked their offer, and it would help him out of his untenable situation.

Hobie got along very well with the new owners and stayed around to help them build the 18- and 33-footers (5.4 m and 10 m). He felt they put in a first rate president, Doug Campbell, from Canada, and that Coleman was the one who really built up the Hobie Company over ten years or more of tenure.

It was a new era when Doug arrived. They got the scissors, cut off his tie, and told him no ties around here! Doug kept the Hobie systems in place, did good work, and never screwed up. He loved to go to the regattas and be part of it all—the perfect man for the job. Doug invited Hobie to accompany him to Florida to check on the progress of the 23 ft. cruiser prototype. It was not going well and Hobie recommended trying to sell it to the original promoters for $10,000. There were, however, no takers, and it was eventually sold to a local dealer for about $1,500

By the late '80s, Hobie was completely out of the company and settled on land he bought with his sale proceeds. He kept in touch with the Hobiecat Company, particularly through his sons, Hobie, Jr. and Jeff, who operate "Hobie Designs," which carries items like clothing, skate boards, sunglasses and accessories.

Part 8 The Olympic rejection

I asked Hobie what stopped the 16 becoming an Olympic class, and whether he felt it helped or hindered the class. He speculated they were wrong in rejecting it, because there were thousands of 16s out there, and no one need buy a new boat or spend a fortune to try for an Olympic berth. He felt the 16 was priced at an affordable level and its standardized rigging was a huge bonus.

When the Tornado became the first Olympic catamaran, Hobie's sons, Jeff and Hobie Jr. thought they would try for a berth. They acquired a couple of Tornados, sailed them for a few months, and went to the Olympic trials. Only the winner qualified and because Hobie Jr. was laying second, he took a gamble which unfortunately placed him fourth behind Jeff. Hobie acknowledged that the Tornado was demanding and had first rate guys sailing her, but his son had been able to place well because there was such a small field. He argued the huge numbers of first class Hobie sailors would eat alive the few Tornado sailors. There are Hobie kids that don't have the money to try for the Olympics, but just the same sail their hearts out. Richard Loufek, a really hot 16 and Prindle sailor, went into the Tornado class and boom, just like that, became their number one skipper. Most big champions start life as dinghy sailors, get really good, and then attract sponsors in any class they want.

In conclusion, Hobie emphasized the 16 should have got into the Olympics, and that would have enhanced the name, but he felt the class would be immeasurably hurt and would be the worst thing that could have happened. After all, how many guys are reasonably hoping to enter the Olympics — one from each country! He said he would hate to manufacture a boat solely to entertain one fellow going to the Olympics. It may be a nice carrot with great prestige, but in the long run the class will be stronger without Olympic status.

I reminded Hobie that Olympic status had not hurt the Laser, and he agreed it worked well as an Olympic boat. Other countries didn't recognize any class that wasn't Olympic, and consequently gave them huge sponsorship, to the detriment of help to other classes. In the States, help from the associations and scholastic bodies is not restricted to Olympic classes. The Hobie 16 never set out to be an Olympic boat. As Arthur Knapp said, if everybody was given a bathtub and a handkerchief for a sail, he would race along with them. Competing with the other guy on an equal basis was the vital point.

But sailboat classes don't go on for ever, and Hobie speculated whether Olympic status would extend the life of the 16 and give it a final kick at the cat. Even so, it seemed to be kicking along on its own. He knew the company supported the Olympic ratification and said he and his family would have been proud of the prestige, but he felt the class would be the winner in the long run as non-Olympic.

I asked Hobie what he thought about the trend to company retail outlets. He said they had excellent dealers, but just the same, he and his partner opened Hobie Sports Centres in downtown Laguna and Dana Point, which handled clothing, accessories, and boards. The stores were eventually sold to other family members and were still going strong. He thought they were much better off with the boats in the hands of the dealer network with its personal interest in promoting the boats. In fact, he felt company stores were not the way to sell boats.

Part 9 Hobie expands outside the United States

The move outside the States started with France and Australia. Denny Keough manufactured surfboards in Australia, and when Hobie noticed the "K" insignia, so similar to the Hobie

The Tornado - the only Olympic catamaran class

Life in the Sailboat World

"H," he saw Denny as a candidate to make the 16. At a world surfing championship, Hobie jokingly accused him of knocking off the insignia. Denny admitted it without guile and expressed a desire to build the long admired 16. Hobie agreed. Denny was licensed to manufacture the 14 for a couple of years to get a good base, and then the 16.

Because of Australia's small population, I wondered if Denny also got the Asian rights. Hobie said, no, but the vast amount of ocean around Australia produced a huge water sport-loving population. He thought they were a bunch of crazy but capable guys, hard to keep up with, and his sons partied with them many times.

The expansion into France came when Hank Pauloo, who had shaped surfboards for Hobie, observed the 16 development in Australia. Hank went to France, married a French general's daughter, and soon after approached Hobie about building the 14 and 16 in France. Hobie happily obliged. He knew Hank was good with fibreglass, knew Hobie's systems, and was one of the stir crazy surfboard guys. None of them were sailors, but they understood the system. Later John Dinsdale went to work for Hank and in 1989 became the majority shareholder of a now independent French company.

All three guys started as surf boarders, were friends of Hobie or worked for him one way or another.

Surfing really got started in Hawaii, spread to the US west coast, and then fanned out to Australia around 1956. France followed, and eventually South Africa fell in behind. In 1964 the great movie, *Endless Summer*, crystallized all the action. Hobie told me about South Africa's John Whitmore, called Mr. Surfing and Mr. Water. John came by to see Hobie while surfing in the States; he was a nice guy and they became great friends. He had known about him earlier because he bought foam from Hobie's contacts. One day John called, said he would like to build the Hobies in South Africa and once again, just like that, it happened.

There was also a Mexican operation aimed at supplying the tourist rental outlets, but it didn't get very big.

Part 10 Lawsuits and other problems

I wondered if the company had ever been pestered with law suits; I had heard they had problems with the pylons working loose, and Hobie told me they fixed that matter and no lawsuit arose from it. However, there was a legal problem with masts and high tension wires, which evolved from the intrinsic success of the boat being able to be launched or taken anywhere. Sailors began launching away from beaches on ramps and other remote areas, and they encountered power lines. People were often so engrossed with their sailing, they didn't pay attention to power lines.

He said there is a story behind each claim; one guy threw a hammer on a rope over a wire to measure the height, but didn't realize the wire was sagging in other places. There was a current and a strong wind; he drifted into the wire and was killed. Another boat ran out of wind near a Florida causeway with no idea which direction to go. They suddenly saw the parking area and the crew jumped off to turn on the car lights as a beacon; while dragging the boat through the trees up a dark, strange beach, they failed to notice the power lines.

Another time in Hawaii on the north shore, the parking lot was busy, so four guys carried their boat to the side of the ramp, around a phone booth and trees, when suddenly the ground became steep. These guys were contractors, and one of them was even watching for wires, but suddenly the boat tilted and the mast hit a wire, killing two of them. When a hull moves a little bit the mast moves a lot, up high. Another guy picked up two girls from the beach, sailed them to his condo, and hit wire at the entrance. He stayed on board, but told the girls to jump off, and both were killed in the water. The safest place when hitting a wire is to stay on the trampoline without touching anything.

The first manual the company put out warned of all kinds of hazards, including "high tension wires." After the first accident, Hobie wanted to put warning stickers on the mast, but the attorneys told him such action would be admitting guilt. Hobie didn't care as long it saved lives and warned the attorneys that if stickers were not implemented, he would prove an ugly witness in court. So, on went a warning sticker near the downhaul, and then a larger one, and it cut down accidents, but not completely.

Most of the strikes were above the shrouds, so the company devised the plastic Comptip for the top of all masts, and that stopped the problem. I told him it was very good thinking, and he wondered why he had not thought of it earlier. He also wondered why the other popular cats didn't instigate this safety feature, as the courts were finding the manufacturers instantly guilty, with no hope of winning a law suit.

Another time, a car was trailering a Hobie with the mast lying in a crutch pointing over the car. It was tied down with a rotten piece of rope that broke. The mast went airborne, through the window of an oncoming car and killed a woman in the back seat. It went through her head and Hobie was dreadfully shocked and upset when they showed him the photos. His lawyers told him he would lose the case: the owner of the trailer had $20,000 insurance; the trailer maker paid; there was some other insurance; and that left the Hobie company responsible for the rest. They had nothing to do with the accident, but in Florida, if you are 1% guilty you can be found 100% responsible. If they can't get anything out of the other parties and the jury sees the photos, the company could be forced into a settlement. The insurance company would pay the claim ,and the company's premiums would increase, like they seemed to do every time something happened.

The cases are all sad: a happy day's sailing and your friend is suddenly dead. Most people are aware of the mast hazard, but just accidentally hit high tension wires. I said I knew of people out in small boats hitting bad weather and perishing, but is that the fault of the boat? They said it could be; they had a case in Tahiti where a fellow moved from one island to the other and decided to gather all his stuff and take it over on the boat. His friends told him he shouldn't do it, and the dealer told him the same thing, but he ended up doing it any way. He hit sudden rough weather and vanished.

Life in the Sailboat World

Hobie recalled one instance which "took the cake" for him. An attorney lay on the trampoline while his buddy skippered his 14. The boat heeled and he slid across the tramp into the shroud adjusters, got a bit scratched up, and sued the company for $50,000. His wife also sued, but for $5,000, and Hobie felt she knew his true value! He said each accident was never a normal, straight deal; nobody meant to do wrong or hurt anyone. He was thankful the Comptip had stopped most of the electrocution lawsuits.

Part 11 Impediments to the sport of sailing and windsurfing

I reminded Hobie a relatively small number sailed and asked him what he thought was the greatest impediment. He promptly replied "the power boat," where you can open up the throttle and take off. Sailing has many mysteries, especially the one of how to make it go into the wind. He thought if the average guy got a chance of a ride on a sailboat, and played around with it a bit, he would soon discover it was fun. Unfortunately, not many get the chance, and this is probably the main reason people don't sail.

A sport needs to be a challenging, pleasurable thing to do, and sailing is very exciting, especially when jumping waves and trying to survive in heavy weather.

I told Hobie that in the eastern states sailors complain about expensive club memberships, land costs, zoning, the shortage of low-cost launching and parking, and the general lack of funding. He said out west the harbours and the few natural bays in populated areas were being eaten up by increasingly private ownership, and that this lack of space very definitely hurts sailing and boating generally. He said Hobie Cats and kayaks were less restricted as long as they could get to a beach, but mentioned even the beaches at coastlines and lakes were being eaten up by increasing private ownership.

The highest number of boat owners were on the east coast, which had the advantage of inland waterways and 994 miles (1,600 km) of warm, 70° F (21° C) summer water, from Miami to Long Island. Florida alone has inland waters, and three coastlines of reasonably calm, warm water, which makes for a lot more sailors. People don't realize that in California, you might have about 200 miles (321.87 km) of 50° F to 60° F (10° C to 15° C) water running south from Point Conception. For a few days you might get 70° F (21° C) degree water, but on average it is not warm at all, and they are out there in wetsuits. This, coupled with scarce good, accessible, or even usable beaches on the Southern California coastline, does not help the sport of sailing.

Lack of coastline explained why Hobie sold 80% of his surf-boards on the east coast. Once they started building good boards there, however, he found it harder to compete because of freight and minimum wage disadvantages.

Part 12 Life after the Hobie Company

I mentioned this interview took place on Hobie's 60 ft. (18 m) power catamaran, which had a 26.3 ft. (8 m) beam and 7,400 lb. (3,356 kg) displacement. He started this magnificent craft around 1988, working in one of the unused Hobie mold shops whose lease was expiring. He planned it as a four-year project and tried to hire skilled guys who were available at the time for his project. He assembled a crew who found everything new, exciting, and fun; none had built a large boat before, including Hobie.

Cats are usually built to a width ratio of 2:1 but his was not so wide, being strictly a power cat. He thought motor sailers were neither good powerboats nor good sailboats unless cruising around the world when there is a need to carry a lot of fuel. Even cruising in the Pacific Northwest demands a motorboat, because the weather can't be depended upon; currents run like crazy, and there are really high winds or no winds. He felt he had absolutely built the right boat, and had cruised from California to Glacier Bay in Alaska. One of the best trips was when he and his wife went from Dana Point, California, to the San Juan Islands, some 1,000 miles (1,600 km) full of little nooks and crannies, which he loved. They were under no deadlines and would stay for a few days in harbour whenever the weather got really nasty. They usually managed about 200 miles (322 km) a day running fast.

Life in the Sailboat World

I asked Hobie what he thought of the new polyethylene Escape sailboats and particularly their Playmate catamaran. He said he hadn't seen it, and even though friends occasionally sent him magazine pieces, he didn't have a lot of knowledge of the current scene. He now lives in a different world. He is building a house, plays golf, and skis. His new life features a tractor out back and a trout pool in the meadow. He loved the surfing, cat sailing, and motor cycling days, but now very much likes his current life, doing new things. He said he was not the type to stick to one thing all his life. He loved to downhill ski all winter, on a local hill with few people and good snow.

He told me he lives straight west of Sun Valley, where they have a small parcel surrounded by state forest and no neighbours. He was able to get the water rights and built the trout pool; I could see he liked fishing.

Part 13 Closing thoughts

I asked him in retrospect if he had any other bright ideas like the Hobie Way of Life, to promote sailing, and he thought it would be hard to repeat that recipe. He thought the best promotion was when sailors and dealers at the Hobie regattas offered, on a volunteer basis, inexpensive sailing lessons. He chuckled, telling me there were so many Hobie Cats in Florida they named one of the causeways the Hobie Beach. In South Africa they asked him if he wanted to visit the Hobie Beach out of Port Elisabeth. He said, "You must be kidding," but it was real. He thought this kind of thing was good promotion, too.

Other classes wanted to mix in with the Hobie groups, but he was always against it. He felt the Hobie guys were doing all the work and should reap the rewards. Besides that, they would have to sail under handicap, which was not popular and never seemed to work. He thought it was more fun if everyone was in the same type of boat and not worrying about the other class being better.

He wanted to get away from the feeling that the boss had a faster boat, so he always raced a stock boat. In fact, the desire to have sailors on an equal basis at the Nationals led the company to supply identical boats and to switch boats after every race.

A fellow who won the first race found he was not winning the second, yet he was in an identical boat. Slowly, the realization dawned on them that it is the sailor who wins races. In fact, Hobie gave them pep talks, trying to convince the guys they had to sail better, but all they wanted to talk about were things to make their boat go faster. He told them the odd thing, but basically preached: learn to sail better, like making good starts and learning to be at the right end of the line.

He said the one thing he was proud of with his children was that he insisted they learn to race correctly. Having a clean boat is fine, but what you really need to know are the tricks of racing and what makes you win, like dealing with wind shifts, planning tactics, and most important, keeping out of dirty air.

One warning he gave was that a group needs to look out for some of its serious sailors, and not let them run the show, because they will gear everything to their needs. They put their full time into racing and don't mind spending more money. They would like all boats to be equal, but their own to be better. A class needs someone to step back and decide what is best for all the sailors. The elite guys cannot be given preference; if you let them just race each other, when it comes time to give out the trophies, there won't be 200 people sitting around having a party and cheering for you. There might be the five elite racers clapping. It is necessary to get everybody involved, and it has to be fun for everyone. A, B, and C groups are a terrific way for a sailor to earn his place up the line.

He recalled originally that the Hobies horned in on the P-Cat races at Lake Havasu, and the P-Cat sailors didn't like it. There were tensions and conflicts, and he didn't blame the P-Cat guys. The Hobies moved their regatta to different weekends. The class was kept simple, and they did a lot of relaxed racing with a good start line, sailing fair by the rules and not nit picking. Most only want a fair shot from competition and to be able to party after with a buddy and tease him he only won because of a good wind shift. The camaraderie achieved is one of life's pleasures, and I truly believe other classes have to build up their numbers and aim for their own thing.

I told Hobie that in our area, even the Hobie Regatta numbers were slipping, and that they invited other cat classes to join them, but with separate starts. It was quite difficult to run two-day regattas as people had so many demands on their time, but everyone was trying to encourage young sailors. Hobie told me years ago the company experimented with an 11½ ft. (3.5 m) cat, which was like a baby 14. It was good for no more than a 100 lbs. (45 km) and perfect for youngsters. Hobie told them it wouldn't make money as it would have to be sold for a low price, but would cost as much as the other boats to produce. He was right, and they dropped it, even though Hobie told them they had all the tooling, could run a

Getting so many boats to regattas is not easy these days with all the demands on people's time and the cost of gas

Life in the Sailboat World

batch in the winter, and get some youngsters into it. He thought this would be almost free promotion to create a new group to move up to the larger Hobies, and still regrets they didn't do it. He felt it hurt the company that they had nothing for training juniors, except crewing for their parents. The recent Hobie Bravo might fill this bill.

Hobie thanked me for my well prepared questions, but believe me, the pleasure was all mine, in spades! I felt even more fortunate when I found he was occupied with so many other things, he had not been able to accept an invitation to speak at the New York Yacht Club. In fact, Hobie confided, while he appreciated being asked, he was not comfortable speaking in public and worried for weeks before any engagement.

The Hobiecat Company continues to forge ahead, particularly in the rotary molding field, with the Wave and Getaway now joined by the Bravo.

The Sailing Game

Chapter 8

A Look Back Into the Future

"Characters" In the Sailboat World

In 1960 I hired Marvin (Marv) Twain, and he stayed for nine years. He was an expert battery repair man and, although I was warned he was of doubtful character, I always felt indebted to war veterans. He had landed at Normandy in June 1944 while I was in occupied Holland. The Dutch still have deep feelings for their Canadian liberators, as well as for the British, Americans, Israelis, and Poles.

Marv was a likable man with a forever smiling face. He was married with three children, but it wasn't long before calls increasingly came in from creditors and collection agencies. I told him this was bad PR for the company and paid off his total debt on his promise to repay me over a period. He kept to the agreement, but later the calls started up again.

Marv, in addition to being an expert battery man, was very handy. He was a big help sealing my dear old Falcon sailboat and was involved with the early assembly and later the building of the Sea Spray cats. I took him on my Flying Kitten cat for his first ever sail and he, too, got bitten by the bug.

He did the sailboat work after hours with the help of his drinking buddy, Tolly Bryant. I was displeased to find empty beer bottles in a barrel of battery acid, obviously hastily thrown in when I appeared on the scene. There was a standing order of no alcohol on the premises, which I strictly enforced. Both batteries and fibreglass chemicals are explosive risks. I suffered further angst when my battery head office notified me the 500 battery inventory was out some 64 units.

I approached Marv and he readily admitted slipping batteries out the back door after hours. He promised he would make it up and indeed paid off about $500 when he suddenly quit to work for a competitive boat business, Smallcraft of Canada Ltd.

It so happened that Smallcraft had seen the success of the Sea Spray and was busy copying it. Marv was able to give all kinds of advice on how a catamaran goes together, or so he thought. He was very handy, but no engineer, and numerous failures brought on many changes, including its name, although we always called it the Copy Cat. In reality, it was hilarious incompetence and soon after, Smallcraft went bankrupt.

Marv moved on to Lethbridge and worked at Harry's scrap yard and, what do you know, before long, it went under. Mr. Harry bitterly asked me why I had not told him about this character. Marv's next move saw him open his own battery shop in Grand Prairie, and when it closed down a couple of years later, a litany of sorrow came from the suppliers left holding the bag. Marv was capable of looking you in the eye and telling an absolute lie, as well as readily admitting guilt and not giving it a second thought. He often told me, with a grimacing and wicked smile, eyes aglitter, that the long Canadian winters gave crooks a chance to dream up new ways to embezzle or find sucker money.

Marv's new angle was to open a sailboat shop just west of Calgary, initially based on copying our three models: Sea Spray (now Firecat), Sesame (now Arrow) and Commodore (now Crossbow). He had a string of fibreglass shops mold his boats, some as far away as Texas and Mexico, all victims of his smooth silver tongue. He would pay for the first load of boats, but then it was "let me sign and accounting will mail you a cheque." The poor fibreglass shop owners smiled as they were being duped.

The sad part was that victimized buyers ended up complaining to us, even crying, but we felt we were not in a position to discuss Marv's shortcomings. We were asked bitterly why we didn't warn them that we knew about Marv and his boats, but we had to consider the legal aspects and prevent the public assuming that we were bad mouthing a competitor.

Probably his supreme "Canadian winter idea" was to approach the federal government's Ministry of Indian and Northern Affairs with a make-work scheme for Aboriginals to build sailboats. The scheme proceeded, and with Marv's system of paying suppliers part of the time, and having virtually free upfront money from Ottawa, he began selling boats at a fraction of what regular builders charged. The make-work scheme boats were marginal at best, but the public readily bought at dirt cheap prices, bearing out Marv's philosophy of a sucker being born every minute. We never took these boats on trade or consignment, but did benefit from repairing them.

The Department of Indian Affairs was smitten by Marv's proposal and put up six figures without a blink. Knowing Marv, we attempted to give our opinion on the proposal, but nobody wanted to listen. Even a national TV programme got into the act, suggesting Marv was a "Prince of Goodness," providing work for Aboriginals. The TV exec refused to listen, too. Nobody checked out the long list of claims at the courthouse, one not more sad or bizarre than the next.

The government finally caught on after several years of bankrolling "Laughing Marv," and his make-work factory came to a grinding halt. Marv blithely moved to different premises in Red Deer, taking with him all the government bought equipment and molds. Disgruntled employees and shortchanged consumers got 10 cents on the dollar for their trouble. Then one day, the Red Deer premises burnt to the ground, and Marv moved on to happier hunting grounds.

He remarried a well situated woman, and life became easier. He went to London to visit a daughter and, while there, lost an argument with a double-decker bus. Some people think he is still alive and well and hiding in London—laughing his head off—naturally!

Fie Hulsker – Mother of the Alberta Sailing Scene

Every so often, a country produces someone outstanding in [its] sailing community, and Canada has such a person in Fie Hulsker. She has been honored by the Canadian Sailing

Fie Hulsker, mother of Alberta sailing, takes a well-deserved break

Association (CYA) and other groups and deserves a place in my memoir. She became a powerhouse team manager, and you might say she provided the infrastructure to bring juniors to the highest levels including contention for the Olympics. After a long stint with the Alberta Sailing Team (AST) she took on the management of a steadily declining Calgary Yacht Club (CYC). She immediately increased membership to unprecedented numbers and instituted a stable scene for members, learners, and racers as well as supervising building expansion. How does she do this?

I often call you the mother of Alberta sailing and I wondered what your first connections with sailboats were?

I was a teenager in Holland and crewed on a 16-footer, but I would say I can barely sail. I had no other involvement until my own children started to sail when about six and eleven and my sister invited us to sail on her Catalina 30 in Desolation Sound. I thought it prudent to teach my children the difference between bow and stern and the basic "rules of the road." I wanted them to take part in the sailing and not just look at the water. It all went from there.

What prompted you to take on management of the Alberta Team and had you done similar work?

I was not satisfied the way things were going with youth sailing in Alberta. I felt I had something to offer and wanted to volunteer or get involved and try out my own expertise. I had worked with teenagers and found I had organizational skills. In fact, I have worked with teenagers most of my life; I was good with them and liked being with them. Kids pick up on that fast, so it was easy to be with them. You need lots of common sense — if we could bottle it we would be richer.

In a nutshell what were you required to do as team manager?

It does not fit in a nutshell! Originally, I was to do fundraising and the logistics, but it developed into hiring a coach, organizing the kids for Alberta trips, and later taking them across Canada and the USA. My role became organizational/logistical, but technically involved getting 25 teenagers from one side of the country to the other, buying their food, and billeting them. I often cooked for everybody.

Did you cook out of a van or in a campground?

Not a campground — it would be too hard to keep them in a tent or stop them wandering off and having adventures. Ultimately, I was responsible to the parents to keep them in a safe environment. In tents you are asking for a lot of trouble. We were always in motels/hotels, billeted with people, or in rented houses. For instance when we went to Kingston, we would often find a house in a student ghetto. If it was not properly equipped, we went to the Salvation Army and bought basic equipment such as plates and utensils. I would set a menu with the kids and then off we went to do grocery shopping. I would cook and prepare lunches on the road so they would have some home comforts. During the travels I felt my big impact was building a national team spirit and giving them confidence, and the kids learned to support my ideas. I used to say what they were learning would enable them to confidently go on vacation with their friends, and be proud of themselves and their boats. They were well supervised and I taught them to rely on each other for support. I taught them about life and life skills.

Do you think you instilled team spirit into them?

Yes. Just last Friday we all got together for an Alberta Sailing Team Party at someone's home. Some of the members had been on the team for several years, and others were newcomers and younger. We spent the evening talking and brought out the log books, which the kids had been keeping since 1993. This was a history of the team and its different generations, backed up with drawings, photos, and funny stories! It was all done by them and it was very seldom that I would write anything. It was meant for them as a history of their time on the team.

Even in winter, we made the sailing team environment a harbour for escape from what was happening in the rest of their lives. These kids were confronting problems of being at the wrong school, in the wrong group, or were being bullied or pressured to do drugs. Then there were the pressures they faced in their family environments. Often some team activity, road trip, or regatta proved a great safety valve, even in winter months with ski trips and skating parties. Sometimes the team went to movies, made excursions to City Hall Plaza, or had a Christmas meal. All this made for continuity when the new sailing season opened.

I used to write scholarship references or encouraged them to apply, even if they felt they didn't have the right marks. I told them if they had an idea they had to go for it, and all they could lose was the stamp. I emphasized they had to have this positive attitude to get on in the world

At summer camps, I did a lot more work with kids about setting their own code of ethics. I instilled [in them that] sportsmanship is very important in sailing and is hard to come by at the competitive level. I felt if they started talking about a personal code of ethics at 12 or 13 years, they could make it work the rest of their lives. I told them to make a bold statement and test it. My theory is that being a teenager will be the best time in their lives and that if they really screw up, they can usually get away with it. Life gets tougher as an adult, but it is expected that teenagers make mistakes; most parents will be really forgiving if their kids are genuinely contrite and learn from their mistakes. So around age 12, if

Life in the Sailboat World

they came out with statements like I will never tell a lie, I tried to teach that there are degrees to this declaration, and that if Mum chooses a graduation dress which you absolutely hate, are you going to say you love it. So then, you get into white lies and what are white lies and are they okay? All this would make them think, and I believe benefited their road to maturity.

Even now when I travel in a city where I know one of my ex-team members is at university, college or working, I will stop and see them. This November I was in Kingston and hooked up with one of the boys studying engineering and took him to dinner. I also saw somebody who had just moved to Toronto and was struggling. I said, let's go for dinner tonight. As you can see I keep in touch with them.

I think you originally asked me what I did on the administrative side. Well, I was producing the newsletters, fundraising, organizing schedules for the whole year, and implementing them. As in any properly working organization, I did a lot of paperwork! A long answer, but yes, a big job.

Another thing I thought had real value even though it was kind of a joke, was that I knew nothing about sailing. Well, I knew something, but with the kids I maintained an aura of not knowing much about racing. They could come off the water and tell me they did some amazing thing, and I would say, well, that's fantastic. This way I could really build up their ego and their spirit. Afterwards, when comparing notes with the coaching staff, I would learn that child made a big mistake at the mark, but with me they could get away with not telling the whole story. So there was beauty in my not knowing much about what happens on the water.

At the same time I did work with kids who had high expectations of themselves in competition. They had set their goals and were upset and depressed when they didn't attain them. So, I spent time making sure they set realistic goals and talking about dream goals versus reality. I kept to ordinary sport psychology and left racing goals to the coach's provenance.

I had to get over [sic] how they would handle a crisis, and to impress on them they were only 15 and still had a lot to learn. I had to impart they could not allow something to be so upsetting that they would have to leave the sport they loved. Sometimes they were upset by parent issues, and they had to be shown thwarting their parents did not solve their dilemma; more likely the parents understood the tensions. Anyway, they got lots to think about and achieved much maturity in sorting it out.

I was always concerned about Mike Simms, one of the higher echelon racers. He once gave a talk to the kids telling them the best race of his life was when he came sixth. Everything was perfect in that race — the boat was perfect, his body was perfect, but there were just some faster people, five of them. He thought those five could have been psychologically stronger, perhaps tacked one iota quicker or maybe their sail was two weeks newer. He would always remember the race was perfect and his boat talked to him as it hummed along. He was subliminally satisfied with sixth place and that he had raced perfectly and had done his very best.

The boat was talking to me?

Yes a lot of people say that. Ryan, my son, always said his Laser II sang to him. It is a very nice thing.

I went to a talk once at CORK (Canadian Olympic Regatta Kingston)) which with Kiel, Germany, and Poole, England, are the world's prime small boat regattas. Huge is the word with some 2,000 to 3,000 entrants in a good year. One of the guest speakers prior to racing was Peter Kepcha, a [hot shot] racer from the States who had won the Youth Worlds. They asked him about tension on his face, how far his mast was raked, and how you should do this and that. He said he twanged his stays and if he heard a certain noise he knew the boat was ready. I always thought that was really fascinating. He didn't even know why his boat went fast, he just felt and heard a certain tension and he knew he had victory in his hands. It was obviously the right thing and he had a very distinguished junior collegiate career in the States.

No doubt the children were inspired or perhaps puzzled. I recently heard a champion talk about foil angles and shapes, but it strikes me so many external factors are involved it is a difficult issue to impart.

That's what is so exciting about sailing–all the unknown factors that have to be coped with.

What is the age of children accepted for the team?

The team is not setup that way, but in actuality the travelling component and learning to race is geared to kids. Adults have their own classifications

Is it possible to join as young as seven or eight?

I am just trying to think, but I recall we took Keamia Rasa and Christopher Whitehouse when they were nine. We took up to 18- or 19-year-olds and, in fact, when the team went to Mexico there were two 20-year-olds. No age restrictions have been set, but logistically, you can't take little ones on the road. They get homesick, and it is much more difficult to look after them. The youngsters are better off at a summer camp or in a yacht club programme. There are dangers in taking a too young child on a road trip, as they don't have experience of totally new environments and are nervous and unsettled. The very nature of living in Western Canada requires the team to make long trips, often as far as the East Coast. These expeditions were spread over four to five weeks, and to have a nine-year-old away from home that long is simply not a good idea. The younger children were kept within the province on smaller projects, with the exception of the Youth Nationals, which I believe to be the premier regatta for Canadian youth. The CYA does an excellent job and includes guest speakers, creating an atmosphere which lets the kids realize there are Canadian champions in their age group and class, and it has enormous value. That whole atmosphere is a humungous motivator for young kids, and we took them even if they were not race ready. The 13- to 14-year age groups are not technically ready to sail at a national event, but I found it very encouraging when the parents were ready to let them go. You can't do that with nine-year-olds as it is too overpowering for them.

What was the average number of regattas and training camps you took the children to each year?

In January and February we went to Florida for the Mid-Winters East at Sarasota, Clearwater, or Miami. Then there would be the Mid-Winters West in California. At spring break in March or April, we would run a week-long training camp on the west coast. Then we would run four training camps in Alberta the last week of April and all of May. Then we did the June Series. We would have a nine-day summer camp at Skeleton Lake. After all this, we would go on the road. We would do the Canadian Youth Nationals wherever they were and tie in two or three regattas like Western Intermediates or Sail West (or Sail East). If the Nationals were in the east we would add CORK (at Kingston). It didn't make sense to drive to, say, Lunenberg, Nova Scotia and come straight back home. We would end up doing at least three regattas on the summer road trip and be on the road 4-6 weeks.

Back in Alberta, we would do the provincials, and the real diehards would enter the Club regattas like the Monkey Barrel, Frostbite, or Thanksgiving near Edmonton. It usually happened after the August provincials — the parents would say that had been enough and sailing gear was to be put away in favour of the new school year. There was a big drop off in September because of school.

So that was our basic schedule, but not every child went to every event. In the beginning, Krysztof, the coach, took the Florida Mid-Winters trip and even that we didn't go to every year. It depended on how much interest there was and if the kids needed that type of competition at their stage of development. We always did a road trip and four clinics within Alberta. Later we frequently did a west coast spring break trip.

It was a pretty full schedule for all of us and was on a pay-as-you-go system. The parents got the registration package in advance and could choose which events did not clash with school exams, as well as tallying up the cost of boat and child transportation in the team's van. The parents wrote the cheque, but most expected their kids do summer jobs to contribute to the sailing schedule costs.

What hard knowledge or value did the children get out of all the regattas?

In my opinion they benefited enormously. The 16 and under Westerns, and the Canadian Youth Championship were choc-a-block full of sailing knowledge and training for kids. Prior to the events, there would be seminars with guest experts to help broaden the horizon or scope of the regatta. As an example, at Youth Nationals we have had a grinder and sail trimmer from the America's Cup covering different aspects of sailing that went beyond the youth circuit. They are valuable not only to teach about the sport, but in giving them role models in a wider world beyond youth sailing.

The biggest problem I see is too much focus on the youth component and not realizing there is a wealth of adult sailing out there, too, which opens the door to many new horizons throughout life. Some think when they are finished with their youth sailing they are all washed up. They don't realize they can sail into their eighties, like Denmark's Paul Elvstrom, perhaps world's most famous sailor, three times Olympic gold medalist and many times World Champion in various classes. He also builds boats, has a sail loft, makes fittings, and writes books. He and his granddaughter sailed in the 1988 Seoul Olympics in a Tornado catamaran when in his early seventies.

So, I still have a chance in my Sea Spray where things are very competitive! I have been invited to join the Laser Masters, but hear it is a backbreaker for the middle aged. I find all the lifting I have done with batteries and boats has given me the strong shoulders necessary to cope with heavy weather sailing.

Life in the Sailboat World

Well, my husband took part in the North American Masters when they were in Red Deer a few years ago, and I think he came 43rd out of 44. He certainly wasn't there to win, but it was one of the few times we could hang out together during the summer as I am mostly on the road. I was his manager/coach, and he really enjoyed the experience. He didn't push himself, and if there was too much wind, he just didn't go out. He was careful of his back; after all, he is in his sixties now and doesn't want to take risks. A group prepared for and went to the World Masters. It was a fun group, and I think any senior sailor could have benefited from it. Most have been consistently competitive racers over the last twenty years but still gain from the coaching and guest speakers.

Did any students have important successes while under your care?

I think the Province of Alberta was the big winner. Alberta started winning at the national level. John Russell and John Driver became Canadian representatives for double-handed sailing at the Worlds in Japan one year. It was a huge moment. They qualified in Laser IIs, but raced in 420s

How did they do there?

They came 13th out of 28 or 29 countries; that is 13th in the world, and I think pretty good. However, that side of it was not really important to me; I couldn't care less if they came 90th; qualifying for the event was the great achievement. They came 2nd in the qualifying Nationals as the team ahead was over the age limit. The following year they actually won the Nationals in Lunenberg and [the] next day hopped on a plane for Japan to represent Canada for a second time at the Worlds.

It looks like we are creating sailing dynasties as both boys had prominent sailing fathers.

It was a very proud moment for me when John Russell and John Driver were chosen. It was well deserved and a great honor for them. The other champion at Lunenberg was Ann Smith in a Laser Radial. It was unfortunate that most of the attention went to the Johns because theirs was a World event. Her performance was outstanding, and I believe she got all bullets [firsts]. In one particular race, she was so fast down wind the coaches from other provinces were stunned by her performance. She was literally on her own, miles ahead, and never lost her concentration. It was a beautiful win, the perfect race if you will.

The other major winner was Mike Simms who got all the way to the Olympic trials only to come second on the last day in the last race. For me it was a great moment, and I am sorry that he did not make it as I always had special feelings about Mike and was proud of the way he ran his campaign. He wasn't all that disappointed and, in fact, spoke to me just after the race, hardly off the water, saying he had given his best, and Marty was just better that day. I like that kind of sportsmanship. Somebody might tell you that does not make winners, but to me that is a winner.

I talk about sportsmanship in this book.

It is hard to find these days. There are other times the kids are total winners, when they overcome something for which they have had great fear. A very sweet moment, like you have given them the stars and the moon. When travelling with kids, you pick up some things are not so great. There is often heartache in families, and kids have big feelings to sort out concerning divorces, parents dying, doing poorly at school, wrong peer groups. Then you travel with them for six weeks and you observe them becoming mentally stronger and you know whatever is going on they will be able to handle it. Being part of that process is very powerful.

Winning can also mean a fantastic start, going from the end to middle of the fleet, or leading for the first time and not knowing the course, and — holy of holies — starting to win. This happened to Laura Alvey at the Woman's Nationals when she was 13 or 14. She slowed down to wait to see where the other boats went and even went the wrong way round the mark. Of course one can never interfere, but she corrected her errors and still won the race! It was a wonderful moment. When I am on the coach boat, I often get teary, because out on the course, they begin to realize their potential and have these great moments. They will always note the course henceforth, and a profound thing like that can be a guide for the rest of their life. Many don't recognize these breakthroughs, but I see them.

Both Laura and Mike gave you great satisfaction.

Yes Mike Simms was in our program since [age] 14 or 15 and is now a young lawyer in Halifax. He did an Olympic try and ran short by one race. It involved dignity, honour, and class, and the actual racing part was minor. When I first knew him, he couldn't organize himself out of a paper bag, was a disaster to travel with, was forgetful, would back into his own boat, and in one classic story, got run over by his own car at CORK. Then to see he finally became a human being who could go from A to B and back to A with all his equipment intact, was probably more of an achievement than going to the Olympics. To me, it was all about life and sailing was almost secondary.

How many kilometres did you put on annually?

We had a few vans and they all had 320,000 to 350,000 kilometres [on them] before we disposed of them, so I suppose we averaged about 5,500 km annually. When seeking van sponsorship, we always claimed we had been round earth three times.

The team existed for about 12 years didn't it?

It began in 1990-91, although there were earlier teams representing Alberta, but not organized the way we were. I talked to Mike Hooper's father at the Calgary Yacht Club (CYC) to get a feel for the history, and he said in the fifties and sixties groups from the club competed at National and North American levels. He mentioned the Leas and Lowneys and the early Lake Sailor, Y Flyer, and Enterprise classes. It was loosely organized, nothing like in the nineties.

My kids joined the team as I was under the impression everyone sailed, but I came to realize it was not a very popular sport. I saw it as a sport that taught life skills and was a good environment for my individualist kids who were not team players per se. My daughter played soccer forever, but only got assists being a right-winger. I think my son had the same result in hockey, so sailing allowed them to individually strive.

Having said that, kids on the team learned to work within a team concept. They all helped each other get along, gave peer support when one had a down day, or helped teammates jury rig boat problems. When we set up the group, we made a conscious effort to make it inclusive as opposed to exclusive. The idea was that kids who came in at ten were mixed with 18-year-olds trying to win Nationals. New youngsters would all be coached and absorbed into the team as one unit. We recognized that a 10-year-old could not sail like an 18-year-old, but then they didn't enter the same competitions. There were no A or B teams, nor any forms of level. The idea was 18-year-olds would learn from the 10-year-olds and vice versa. It was done by a sort of osmosis and it worked for a very long time. I believe it would still work today and was an excellent concept.

What kind of things can an 18-year-old learn from a 10-year-old?

Well, they learn patience and that the fears they overcame at 10 can be translated into fears they must overcome at 18. They all worry as to whether they will be good enough. Except [that], with 10-year-olds, there are no layers yet, and their personalities are not hiding conflicts. Kids are great that way, kind of pure. A 10-year-old often has a really different way of thinking about sailing, because he is so new to the game and is akin to thinking outside the envelope. Perhaps they are sitting on the wrong side of the boat, but they feel they go faster this way. An 18-year-old has been told not to sit on that side of the boat, but when he sees the 10-year-old do it, he tries it, too. Older kids will often mimic 10-year-olds to find out why the kid is moving so well. Sometimes kids can be really direct. You can come up with a fine theory on why you won a race, but a 10-year-old will tell you it's bogus or totally ridiculous, and you are brought back to earth. The children learned compassion and were always rooting for the younger kids or looking out for them. It was like having a young sibling who didn't fight with them. For instance, when an older kid had a really bad day, a 10-year-old would say "that's okay, you are still my hero." It was sometimes enough to get the teenager laughing again and moving on. It is just there—you have to see it.

During your tenure would you rate the Alberta Team near the top or did you feel other provinces were attaining higher goals?

In the beginning our structure was very different from other provinces, because we are so small. For instance, we do not have a Royal Victoria or Vancouver Yacht Club with [its] own racing teams. Basically, we have cottage area small clubs, and there is no way even our largest clubs (Calgary, Glenmore, Wabamum, Brooks) could support a child on an Olympic or National Team campaign. This translates into the British Columbia Team being comprised of the major club members getting together for one-time tries, say, for the Nationals. The fact of the matter is, often they didn't know each other and had just met at the airport. That never seemed right to me, as I thought in a team structure, you should be a team like in Alberta knowing each other, training, and playing together and even meeting over winter. Having said that, it is very hard on a national level to beat provinces like British Columbia or Ontario. It is a numbers game, with tons of money being poured into the club youth sailing structures. The Alberta team finds itself having to beat the strong provinces at the major events.

I always thought Alberta was right behind the strong teams.

The fight was always with the rest of the country for third spot, and here we were very successful, but it was hard to overtake them. The major problem is everything is always so far away and it takes so much effort and coming and going to make the challenges. Before Alberta built up its strength, Manitoba was always the strong province, with an excellent and successful program run by Johnny Burns. A legend grew up around him, and he made sailing the number one sport in Manitoba. He got tons of funding and we couldn't figure out how. Then Manitoba slid into a decline, fractured, and broke apart. A very strong Alberta came on the scene and filled the void, but from time to time you would see Quebec or Nova Scotia in the spot, a continual ebb and flow.

We are nearing the end, but I wondered what makes Fie tick.

Fie was a famous letter writer and at an [sic] age of six she already kept a journal. To this day, I send letters to my whole family, telling about our children and their activities, and I suppose they became a picture of how we raised our children. My relatives returned some letters I wrote 22 years ago, and my children, in turn, got a picture of my youth. It is lovely to read how I felt at sixteen and it truly helps me to understand today's 16-year-olds. Things don't change. I find myself being able to talk at their level and commiserate, especially as I had a terrible time with my mother, 'til I was about 19.

She was a very difficult human being and a challenge every morning I got up. I had to say she will not get me down today. She was a tough cookie; she was negative and unhappy and seemed to take everything out on me. Now, I can see it built my character and I am grateful. Years later, we had a wonderful relationship, when I came to understood she had difficulties with health, marriage, and finances. So I don't argue with my children, just try to show them the big picture.

Kids would put themselves down with "I am not pretty, not smart, won't amount to anything." I tell them you can see I am overweight and if I had let it bother me I wouldn't have got out of my crib. I was a 12-lb baby and was not going to hide underneath a rock. My size has never held me back or counted against me, and I tell them they have to live with what they are and compensate an ugly nose with a big heart, that somebody will fall for them! I continually told kids not to get excited about these things, but look at the big picture. Many children came to say I was absolutely right, and they ended up doing a lot better. I think I gave that to them.

Do you consciously help your children avoid the struggles you had, especially with your mother?

I have always had a great and honest relationship with my

kids. Communication in our family is a big thing. When I couldn't reach them with common sense, I did so with humor and taught them to laugh at themselves. My son, Ryan, told me he didn't get into trouble as a teenager because he couldn't bear to disappoint or hurt us. He didn't want us to think less of him or to shake our solid family foundation. I found there are lots of kids who don't respect their parents and consequently have no brake on their natural impulses. They don't give a damn what their parents think, so they just go and do it.

I felt I was given too much responsibility, and it took away some joy from my teenage years. I probably live vicariously through my sailing kids—who knows. My mum was very ill when I was 13½ and near death. She was hospitalized for six months, and I took over the running of the household, which included paying the bills, cleaning, looking after younger brothers, cooking three meals a day, giving Dad a lunch and spending money, and making sure he got to work in time. I was shattered when my mother came home and declared she would never run the household again and was going out to work. She claimed as I had done such a good job, I could keep it up, so at 14, I kept cooking, cleaning, and all that. My Dad was also shattered; he was born in 1905 and having a working wife at a time when women generally didn't work was hard on him. It was a huge task for a 14-year-old, but it was the basis for the organization and talent required in later years in the Alberta Sailing Team, political jobs, and running sailing clubs.

Employees and Managers

Personnel in any business can be a godsend or minions of the devil. We had some wonderful employees who were helpful, cheerful, never minded putting in extra hours, and always produced good work.

Hans Kreuz, Duuk van Heel, and later Willem Leijs and Gary Lee, would sometimes work until midnight to get a client's boat ready or prepared for a regatta. The staff doubled up their boats on inverters, tied them down well, drove hell bent at least 400 miles (650 km) after work through the night to a major regatta, such as Kelowna. Time for a quick shower on arrival at our favorite Caravelle hotel overlooking the race course, a quick rig, and there we were at the starting line in time for the first gun with our Flying Kittens and Sea Sprays.

I recall one Sea Spray sailor, a wonderful Australian, named Phil Ryan, so tired that he fell asleep on his trampoline waiting for the start. He regularly woke to the blast of the starting gun, asked dazedly which way, and went on to place well!

Duuk, Hans, Willem, and Martin also produced procedure manuals, which greatly benefited our company. Employees could refer to methods of construction, rigging, and "go fast" specialized systems. The words barber haulers, travelers, Highfield levers, boomvangs, and Cunninghams were a foreign language to new employees.[1]

We enjoyed employees who could produce a smile, and were open to advice and new ideas, or gave guidance to new staff. These kinds of people make companies successful, but you would be surprised how many react by being irritated, getting mad, or walking out—too lazy to absorb new ideas. We tried to treat people like human beings and pay them well. We offered them the use of sailboats and, in good years, rewarded them with a healthy bonus.

Wages are quite basic in the sailboat industry, and we had to compete against oil industry rates. Building boats is very labour intensive, but the consumer, generally, is not willing to pay more. He will pay high figures for powerboats and skidoos, but some-

---

[1] **barber haulers** (brings the jib closer to the centre line to help pointing closer into the wind); **travelers** (gives improved sail settings and better control over heeling); **Highfield levers** (tensions the leading edge of a sail, which puts the draft further back);**boomvangs and cunninghams** (mainsail aft draft controls; used to deal with increasing tension on the sails as the wind blows harder and harder)

Life in the Sailboat World

Trying to catch Phill Ryan, famous for waking up at the start gun

how a sailboat is often a second class citizen. In order to survive, we became efficient purchasers and did not allow our margins to be affected by even one percent. There is no high living in this industry, and one constantly watches overhead and ever increasing expenses. In early days, we didn't need to accept credit

Life in the Sailboat World

cards, but the scene changed, Eventually we had to absorb credit and bank card expenses, higher utilities, taxes and transportation costs, fancy promotions, and charitable demands. With no pun intended, one has to run a tight ship, and I believe ignoring mundane controls has caused many failures in this business. Government costs at all levels are probably equivalent to being the largest shareholder.

It is all a matter of give and take, and too many preferred the take side. I remember one engineering student saying he wanted to have it out with me. I agreed to sit down after closing, and it turned out he did not want to do menial jobs like packing, vacuuming, dusting, and washing boats. I told him even generals start as soldiers and that it is valuable to know how things work efficiently at all levels so one can judge an employee's performance. He was a bright student, and we had no trouble with him the rest of the summer. He worked out so well that when he went back to university we gave him a bonus.

And then there were the four aboriginals who took off to see Prince Charles sign the Treaty of Seven and never came back! The Vietnamese fellows did good work, but when criticized by the production manager, claimed Fred had told them to do it that way. Some employees used old or fictitious invoices and pocketed the proceeds, which works well until somebody comes back for a refund. Others shoved masts or trailers over the fence after hours. One bright spark took an 18-footer (5.49 m) out to demonstrate while we were away, sold it, and pocketed the funds. This one had the grace to quit and pay up when threatened with the law.

There were also employees who, at the drop of a hat, complained to the Labour Relations Board. There were few serious employee disputes, but we were always found to be not at fault. Sometimes, employees get hot under the collar and don't check their facts.

We had been employers for many years and felt we had the staff's interest at heart and a desire to meet the requirements of the law to the last letter. It annoyed us to find staff slacking off when we were away, but I suppose it is a universal problem. There were those who felt it okay to drape their legs over my desk, use the photocopier ad infinitum, make interminable personal calls, or study web pornography. Sooner or later, one always finds out, including one charming fellow we caught wining and dining his girl friends on the company credit card. "Just take it out of my wages," he said with a smile. That was his last pay cheque.

Only once did a client take us to court over a repair problem. It was a complicated issue, but our brilliant lawyer managed to convince the court the client caused the problem by trailering his boat with the mast up and hitting an overhead wire. At the end of the trial, the judge asked one of our men if he would do the repair the same way again and he answered, "Oh, no, Your Honour," We lost the case right there. Employees are not required to make up losses, but it always heartened us when some staff offered to compensate in some personal way.

We had an excellent Dutch manager at one time, Willem Leijs, certainly capable enough to inherit our company. He loved taking huge loads to Toronto, together with his wife. We used to travel east through the Northern States where roads were better and gas, motels, and food much cheaper. Willem's trip went well, and I was enjoying the fact it was not me on the road for once. Then, the heart stopping phone call came: Willem reported near Chicago that the 6 in. (15.24 cm) steel V-tongue had snapped, and the trailer had careened off the double lane highway into the ditch. The impact caused the top Laser to break its tie downs and become airborne. It landed in a swamp by the freeway, but with not a scratch to be seen! The rest of the boats had not moved an inch, and Willem coolly arranged a tow, had the tongue welded, and delivered the boats. We somehow neglected to tell the Laser owner of his boat's magnificent performance. Willem went back to Holland and became a very successful businessman.

Conclusions About Employees

I have long had a feeling our schools were not preparing people for real life in the business world; my experiences over the years read like a comedy sketch. I found a great many people who could not spell, could not do simple day-to-day paperwork, or pack parcels (a great art!), never mind inserting the correct articles. Then there were those who came late or left early.

Many couldn't see what needed to be done on the most basic levels, and self starters were few. They couldn't even look alert (actually being alert was beyond them). Some could not figure out people just did not want to see their cracks, breasts, or up their legs—nor smell what they ate for lunch or dirty sock fumes. The first clue usually came as I realized they didn't look people in the eyes when talking or listening.

Then, there were those bright sparks who, despite an inability to speak and write adequately, thought they could become CEO in a week. These I usually had to give extra coaching in how to handle basic tools.

Lastly, there were those who denied they had made some glaring error. These ones made you nervous. You never knew where you are with an employee who fibs.

Can it be the schools? I hear about large classes, but that doesn't seem to hinder European kids, often in classes of fifty, who manage to learn basic spelling, grammar, and arithmetic without a calculator. I cannot fathom where the art of spelling got lost—it can't be just the computer. We often hear that computers are down, but I think it's our education.

Future Beach – A Company for the Future

David Lehktman, the wunderkind Future Beach leader had designed and built the Russian pavilions at the World Expositions in Montreal, Spokane, and Osaka. More and more wonderful and innovative products rolled off the desk of this designer who could not keep up with his own brilliance. There were enormous product problems, probably because they were rolling off the line so quickly; there was no time for thorough testing. Sometimes as many as three snarly customers were lined up at the door Monday morning. We would pacify them with quick repairs or new product, with incredible backing from Future Beach. Soon we were helping with product testing, including the near-sinking of a four-person pedal boat and the inversion of a Barracuda water bike. Sales were incredible and affixing Made in Canada stickers and Coastguard numbers came as an afterthought!

By now, Glenmore was carrying at least 51 different water toys from several manufacturers. We had a strong hold on this market, which depended so much on maintaining a reputation for service, service, service. Future Beach capped its success by going public, and one of the Quebec unions held a substantial investment in the company.

Steve Oles told me repeatedly that Future Beach would not sell through distributors, but the old nightmare of huge numbers of rotary molded product rolling off the line reared its ugly head. It was a real surprise when they set up our old friend, the Huston-Barrett Group, who agreed to grandfather Glenmore pricing for a year.

The task of a distributor is to set up a high number of dealers and, in a nutshell, this meant that Glenmore would lose its exclusivity in Calgary and Edmonton and lose major customers throughout Western Canada. I knew this was a bad move, but my gut told me we would overcome in the long run. Once again, it boiled down to expertise and knowledge of product. We knew the distributor did not want to deal with all the pesky problems that come with high use products, and their margin certainly didn't allow for it. Indeed, by 2002 Huston offered Glenmore their entire inventory.

I understood Future Beach had to protect its position by finding more markets, but distributorship didn't seem to be the answer.

A Blueprint for 40 Years'
Survival in the Sailboat Industry

The cyclical sailboat business is space and labour intensive and needs a healthy margin to survive. Profit cannot be thought a dirty word. It is necessary to have a wide product mix and give service, service, and more service. We also had the advantage of being able to manufacture some of our own products. We strongly believed in staying open year round, and that knowledgeable employees pave the road to success. In later years, we sold product all over the world by having an early web site. Orders came in as we slept. We felt, buyer or not, anyone entering the store or even phoning should be given a warm fuzzy feeling. People simply won't come back again if their reception was not friendly on the first visit.

The other vital components are:
1) a chandlery with thousands of fittings, spars and sails always in stock
2) a top notch repair department
3) having customized trailers and dollies available
4) selling on consignment or selling used boats in good condition and representing them accurately
5) keeping promises made and sticking to delivery dates
6) maintaining rigid administration and financial controls

Trying to stay open 24/7 drains a small company, and we thought six-day weeks should do the job. We closed on all statutory holidays and tried to stick to eight-hour days. In season, we did a few extra hours and always offered to stay open for out-of-towners. We thought the cost of staying open longer hours did not warrant the extra expense.

We had a minimum overhead cost of at least $1,000 a day, whether or not we opened the front door. Profits must cover expenses and buy inventory, so it is vital to charge properly and learn accurate costing. Your sales base must be continually extended to keep up with products that fall away. You must be able to draw on a population base of at least 500,000, as so few people sail or kayak or pedal boat. The business must have a storefront, a workshop, covered storage, and a fenced yard. Working capital or a line of credit of no less than $50,000 and preferably $80,000 should be at your disposal. Access to water is, of course, vital, and it has been a great boon in the City of Calgary that many new subdivisions are built around man-made lakes.

We made it a way of life to have orders out the same day or, at worst, within 24 hours. Such simple action created no end of goodwill and repeat orders. And the final advice is—you must recognize that sloppy paperwork will catch up with you.

The Selling of Glenmore Sailboats

We loved the continual challenge of operating a business and hardly noticed the years passing, or as Frank Sinatra said, we thought it would never end. Little clues bounce around; suddenly 60-plus hours a week is demanding and by 3 p.m. we would be happy to go home. I took a daily 20-minute power nap on a small cot in my upper office, but even this was not enough. We made a point of staying in shape and eating well, which enabled us to work like dogs most of our life. We did 6- to 12-mile-hikes (10 to 20 km) in town or the Rockies most weekends or went for long cycle rides on our very old Raleigh and CCM bikes. We also floated down local rivers to refresh our spirits among the milling birds, beavers, deer, and jumping fish.

We tried to see the world each fall when things were quieter. Most trips centred on visiting famous art galleries or hiking new terrain. We used the local bus or train to get the feel of countries and walked for hours in Paris, Moscow, St. Petersburg, Madrid, Seville, Florence London, New York, Helsinki, Melbourne, Nice, Amsterdam, Bilbao, and Auckland.

Some fifteen years earlier, we thought we might like to sell the company, but did not make a serious effort. In 2001, we were ready to retire and, although Audrey was reticent, I began networking, and several customers who were business brokers gave us help. Ours was an interesting business, but it was often difficult to describe the complexities. In late June, Gordon van Gunst called, asking if it was true we wanted to sell. Gordon, an avid sailor and cadet in his youth, had always dreamed of being in the sailboat business, but his children were still very young. He expressed interest, and we arranged a meeting within 48 hours. Gordon, who has Dutch parents, understood "Boter bij de vis" which translates into, "Let's get down to the nitty gritty."

We had coffee in Gordon and Sheri's beautiful new three storey Lake Chestermere home, which they showed us with pride; it ultimately helped them buy our business. Gordon and his Dad, without any experience, had built the house, while Sheri looked after financing and paying the bills. They both felt it was good training ground for operating a business. Sheri, a registered nurse, was also working on a master's degree while at the hospital.

That evening, we tried to explain the boat business, and figures were bounced around. We made it clear any purchase would require about 80% down. They offered to pay the balance in one year, but we felt two years would be easier at a modest interest rate. We offered to stay without pay for the first three months, help at boat shows, and give counsel when requested. We urged them to complete the deal quickly and get the current summer's income needed to help them through the long, cold winter.

They were realistic, straight forward and had the old fashioned morals in which we believed. They were the kind of people we liked to deal with at the best of times. We agreed to meet again to iron out details, hand over financial records, and sign confidentiality papers. We each appointed lawyers and accountants.

Then came a nerve wracking period I could hardly comprehend. The principals were on the same track, but the lawyers and accountants got in a tizzy with each other and with us. Our accountant of 30 years threw us for a loop and our lawyer, in an effort to protect us, made life very complicated. Legal papers, agreements, offers, and counter offers went flying back and forth week after week. We were all losing our patience and often met for a snack to ease the tension. Happily, there was still goodwill and intent between us, and finally Sheri told her lawyer to prepare final papers so the bloody deal could be signed and go ahead. We told our people the same thing. And it came to pass that the largest business deal of our lives was signed effective August 1, 2001, and the subsequent two payments were made on the dot.

We feel the purchase is already a terrific success for the new owners. They have significantly increased sales and made good strategic moves in expanding the showroom, widening product bases, switching to a top notch integrated accounting system, incorporating inventory control and lots more. Redevelopment of the downtown site has prompted new land to be purchased and, in due course, modern premises will arise. There has been terrific cooperation and mutual trust from both sides and an intense desire to carry the Glenmore Sailboats' mission forward. I see that youth is the key to the energy and determination needed for continuing success. My Dutch family recently celebrated 250 years of the family business, and I see no reason for the van Gunst heirs not to do the same, making a good start with their three children!

The End

Fred van Zuiden was born in Holland in November 1930, and at the age of eleven had to learn how to survive in his occupied homeland. He found himself in the middle of the Battle of Arnhem, and has had a keen interest in WWII military history since then.

The war years took their toll, and, at age 21, he emigrated to Canada. He lived in Montreal, Toronto, Victoria and Vancouver and took management training. He was an early Hudson's Bay Company Department Head. In the fifties, he accepted a position in Calgary to open a new battery retail outlet. The batteries were a success, and his employer allowed him to build sailboats in his down time. This sideline later evolved as Glenmore Sailboats, from which this story emanates.